Strengths-Based Approaches to Educating All Learners with Disabilities

MICHAEL L. WEHMEYER

Strengths-Based Approaches to Educating All Learners with Disabilities

BEYOND SPECIAL EDUCATION

TEACHERS COLLEGE PRESS

TEACHERS COLLEGE | COLUMBIA UNIVERSITY
NEW YORK AND LONDON

Published by Teachers College Press, 1234 Amsterdam Avenue, New York, NY 10027

Copyright © 2019 by Teachers College, Columbia University

Cover photo by FG Trade / Getty Images. Cover design by Patricia Palao.

Library of Congress Cataloging-in-Publication Data is available at loc.gov

ISBN 978-0-8077-6122-9 (paper)
ISBN 978-0-8077-6164-9 (hardcover)
ISBN 978-0-8077-7764-0 (ebook)

Printed on acid-free paper
Manufactured in the United States of America

26   25   24   23   22   21   20   19   8   7   6   5   4   3   2   1

This book is dedicated to the memory of two of my mentors: William W. Zimmerman, EdD, my undergraduate advisor, whose enthusiasm and passion for special education was infectious; and Ernest A. Gotts, PhD, my doctoral advisor, whose kindness was surpassed only by his encyclopedic knowledge. Both are now gone, but I hope their legacy continues through my work.

Contents

Introduction

Why Change?

This book is written not as a critique of special education as it exists today. It is written with the intent to put forward some big ideas about how the education of learners with disabilities can be structured in the future. It has been more than 40 years since the passage of Public Law (P.L.) 94-142: The Education for All Handicapped Children Act. I had the honor of speaking at the 40th anniversary celebration of what we now call the Individuals with Disabilities Education Act (IDEA) in 2015 hosted by leadership in the U.S. Department of Education's Office of Special Education and Rehabilitation Services and Office of Special Education Programs, the latter of which is responsible for the full implementation of IDEA.

That event provided me an opportunity to consider all that had happened in those 40 years. As a special educator who entered the field only 5 years after the law was passed and 2 years after it had to be fully implemented (1978), I have had the chance to observe, first hand, the impact of this important civil rights legislation. By any indicator, the passage of P.L. 94-142 was a watershed moment for students who had been left out of the education system before its adoption by Congress. I personally remember adolescents with severe disabilities coming to school, into my classroom in Irving, Texas, for the very first time in their lives.

Further, P.L. 94-142 did more than simply open the school door; from the beginning, the law prioritized educating learners with disabilities alongside their nondisabled peers in general education settings. The least restrictive environment language as it was written originally in P.L. 94-142 and as it exists today in IDEA varies slightly, but the intent has not changed: that children with disabilities be educated in regular classes with their nondisabled peers, with the specially designed instruction and supplementary aids and services they need in order to succeed.

I have had the privilege of meeting and getting to know a number of the people who were instrumental in the passage of P.L. 94-142, who litigated the cases that led to the Act, and who helped craft the language in it. We have talked about elements of the Act that played out differently than they anticipated. I'm of the impression, for example, that they never intended for the individualized education program (IEP) requirements to become such a contentious, bureaucratic process. But, I'm sure if you asked them whether they were proud of the accomplishment, their unanimous response would be yes.

I also have known people with disabilities who came of age before 1975 and were denied the right to a free, appropriate public education. I was reminded as I talked with and listened to them that IDEA was and is, fundamentally, a civil rights act on a par with the Civil Rights Act of 1965. In landmark civil rights cases on behalf of children with intellectual disability and their families leading up to P.L. 94-142, the courts interpreted the due process clause of the 14th Amendment as requiring equal protection under the law with regard to the right to education for all. It is not coincidental or trivial that the 14th Amendment was adopted in the wake of the Civil War and the passage of the Civil Rights Act of 1866, and has been used to ensure citizenship rights and equal protection in situations ranging from the rights of former slaves, to women's voting rights, to the inherent inequality of racially segregated public schools, and, yes, to IDEA's assurance of access to a free, appropriate public education for all students. For children and youth with disabilities and their families, IDEA is, indeed, first and foremost a civil rights act.

No, this book is not intended as a response to the current law or system. Are there improvements to special education as we know it today that need to occur? Yes, certainly. But that is not what compels me to write this book. Let's celebrate the incredible achievement that 40-plus years of IDEA deserves.

But, let's also recognize that 40-plus years is a long time. There have been fundamental changes to the family, American culture, society, and to schools and the children who go to them since Gerald Ford inked his name on P.L. 94-142. For one, the number of children served under IDEA has doubled since the 1976–1977 school year, from just over 3.5 million children with disabilities ages 3–21 to just under 7 million students in 2015–2016. In 1972, 78% of American K–12 schoolchildren were White. In 2013, that percentage was 50%, and the National Center for Education Statistics predicts that by 2025, it will be down to 46%. Meanwhile, it is estimated that Hispanic children, who made up only 6% of students in public schools in 1972, will constitute 29% of the students in public schools in 2025 (nces. ed.gov/programs/raceindicators/indicator_rbb.asp). In 2015–2016, 16% of all children receiving special education services (as a percentage of total enrollment in public schools) were African American, surpassed only by American Indian/Alaska Native children at 17% (nces.ed.gov/programs/coe/indicator_cgg.asp). Both are highly disproportional compared with the percent of African American or American Indian/Alaska Native children in the total school population (only 15% and 1%, respectively).

Or, consider the digital revolution. A single tablet PC today has the computing power equivalent to 5,000 desktop computers in 1985 (Schwab,

2017). Personal computing didn't exist in 1975, nor did personal access to the Internet. Technology wasn't a consideration, fundamentally, in P.L. 94-142.

And, let's face it, the framers of P.L. 94-142 were working from an incomplete knowledge and experience base. In the 150 years leading up to 1975, the country had warehoused, sterilized, segregated, and legally discriminated against people just like the children the law was now seeking to include in public schools. The Americans with Disabilities Act, affording Americans with disabilities full protection from discrimination and ensuring equal access to the benefits of society, wasn't even passed until 16 years after P.L. 94-142 came into existence. The John F. Kennedy administration provided the first serious impetus to community inclusion for children with disabilities—and in many ways P.L. 94-142 was the crowning achievement of the parent movement spawned by the Kennedy initiatives. However, the institution census in America for people with intellectual disability did not peak until 1979, when more than 250,000 children, youth, and adults were institutionalized in state-run facilities. P.L. 94-142 was amazingly progressive in its call for the education of learners with disabilities alongside their nondisabled peers; still, the primary models that the framers and early special educators had to work from were segregated models.

So, this book is written not as a criticism of existing special education or of the existing federal law. But, 40-plus years is a long time. Much has changed in society and education. This book is written to examine ideas for going "beyond" special education in the sense of looking at some of the big ideas that should drive future educational experiences for learners with disabilities. Some of these ideas have been discussed quite broadly; others remain under the radar. The ideas are not necessarily my own. I can't even claim originality for the subtitle of this book. In 1987, pioneering special educators Alan Gartner and Dorothy Kerzner Lipsky published a paper in the *Harvard Educational Review* titled "Beyond Special Education Toward a Quality System for All Students." That article was a reflection on 10 years of the implementation of P.L. 94-142, and the authors presented their recommendation for the Regular Education Initiative, criticizing the separate special education system and arguing for a single education system for all children. Gartner and Lipsky's seminal paper was, clearly, a critique of existing law and a challenge to change the system. I suppose any effort to effect change is, at least nominally, critical of efforts that preceded it. But that is not my primary focus. And, while most of the ideas are not mine originally, I hope that because of my experiences I am able to synthesize knowledge and information to take those ideas forward in ways that might be at least thought provoking.

So, why write this book? Why change? Because it's 2019. Everything else has changed. It's not even like everything that is in P.L. 94-142 was invented from whole cloth in 1975. The Council for Exceptional Children

(CEC), which of course is the field's most visible professional association, held its 53rd annual conference in 1975, so there was already a half-century of practice in special education when P.L. 94-142 was passed. Many of the ideas codified in P.L. 94-142 go back years before the law was enacted. The federal Bureau of Education for the Handicapped (the precursor to the Office of Special Education Programs [OSEP]) preceded P.L. 94-142 by almost a decade (it was established in 1967). Congress passed the Education of the Handicapped Act (P.L. 91-230) in 1970, providing grants to stimulate states to implement special education. In an editorial to a 1977 article discussing the importance of P.L. 94-142, Fred Weintraub, who as head of Governmental Relations for CEC at that time had a lot to do with crafting the law and getting it passed, stated that the Act "is not revolutionary in terms of what it requires nor is it revolutionary in terms of a role for the federal government" (p. 114). P.L. 94-142 was the cumulative effort of what was known from at least the mid-1960s onward.

I also recognize that the Act has been reauthorized and updated periodically to address critical societal and educational issues that have arisen since its passage and to infuse innovative ideas and practices into it, but the fact is that much of the structure of P.L. 94-142 remains the same, for good or for ill. But, 2019 is not 1975. In many ways, it's not even 1999 or 2009. The rate of change has increased. It is time to look at how we might structure the education of learners from 2020 and beyond.

There are two other topics that belong in this Introduction. First, my career has been focused mostly on the education of learners with intellectual and developmental disabilities, although through our research we have worked extensively with students with learning disabilities and, to lesser degrees, students across all other disability categories. My thoughts in this volume will, necessarily, be influenced by my experiences. And, I would argue, it was mainly the students that I have worked with who were the impetus for P.L. 94-142, although not the sole beneficiaries. But, it is my experience that the issues I raise have a universality across disability categories and, indeed, across children, so I attempt to speak about all children and not just the children I have worked with most closely.

And, I have already mentioned my own experiences as influencing what will be in this book. Among the pioneers in the field of intellectual disability, in which, as I mentioned, I have spent much of my career, was psychologist Seymour Sarason. Known primarily as the founder of the Yale Psycho-Educational Clinic and as a pioneer in community psychology, Sarason was important to the field of intellectual disability at a critical juncture in its development. Sarason had worked for several years at a state institution for people with intellectual disability, and that experience taught him a great deal about the importance of context in understanding human development. Sarason was among the first researchers to emphasize the role of context in conceptualizing disability, writing in 1985 that "mental retardation is never a thing or a characteristic of an individual, but rather a social invention stemming from time-bound societal values and ideology that makes diagnosis and management seem both necessary and socially desirable" (p. 233). It took the field almost 3 decades to catch up, but current conceptualizations of intellectual disability emphasize person–environment fit or social–ecological factors.

I bring up Seymour Sarason because when I consider what books most influenced me, professionally, over the past 2 decades, I see that several were relatively short books addressing issues that were critical to the field at the time they were published. Not coincidentally, many of these were authored by Sarason. I'm thinking particularly of *The Predictable Failure of Educational Reform: Can We Change Course Before It's Too Late?*, written in 1990; *Revisiting "The Culture of the School and the Problem of Change,"* written in 1996; and *Charter Schools: Another Flawed Educational Reform* and *Political Leadership and Educational Failure*, both written in 1998. What made these books relevant and memorable to me was that (a) they were written by an author with clear credentials but were very readable, not overly burdened by the minutia of typical academic scholarship; (b) they addressed very timely topics when those topics were most relevant; and (c) they were readable not only because of their writing style, but because they were relatively short and could be read quickly.

I don't claim to have Sarason's wisdom or credibility. I do claim to have 40 years of practice in the field in the roles of a direct support worker, a special educator, a researcher, a teacher-trainer, and, throughout that time, an advocate. This book is written in the same tradition as Sarason's books. I believe that multiple forces are merging to create an opportunity to fundamentally change how learners with disabilities are educated and to move us beyond "special education" as we know it today. Strengths-based approaches to disability are moving education away from a focus on diagnosis and remediation to a focus on schoolwide instruction for all students, characterized by features of personalizable education, and incorporating the role of technology, student-directed and self-determined learning, and technology-driven assessment linked to instructional decisions. I hope not to overburden this book with professional citations, but will work hard to ensure that statements I make are grounded in fact as well as my personal experience. To the degree that this short book makes you think about how things are done and what might change, it will have served its purpose.

CHAPTER 1

Beyond Disability

Strengths-Based Approaches
to Educating All Learners

Let's begin by considering how disability was understood in 1975 and how changes in the way we have thought about disability over the past 2 decades might require us to change our practices and to consider going beyond "disability." Special education was established because some students with disabilities did not have access to school, and those who did were not benefiting from standard educational practices. In a 1976 issue of *Exceptional Children*, Lance identified the reason for the establishment of special education as "the recognition of the need to provide different treatments to individuals with obviously differing capacities for benefiting from the traditional educational practices" (p. 68). Lance cited a 1974 resolution from the Council for Exceptional Children that called for the passage of equal access to education legislation by Congress; the resolution stated that children who did not have such access were "children for whom educators have responsibilities to assist in prevention of further injury and to provide programs to remediate the damage that has occurred" (p. 72).

Lance's article and the resolution he cited are fairly typical of the way in which the purpose of special education was presented in the mid-1970s. I want to pull out three words from those quotes for you to think about: (1) treatment, (2) prevention, and (3) injury.

When I was doing my undergraduate training in special education in the late 1970s, I was taught that the educational model differed from the medical model in that the purpose of the former was to fix, remediate, and educate, while the purpose of the latter was to diagnose, treat, and cure. Let's be clear: Even in 1975 the field was not of one mind with regard to the utility of the application of the medical model to special education. But the arguments were about the applicability of medical processes to educational *practices*.

What wasn't in dispute was that how "disability" itself was understood was unquestionably tied to the medical model. The textbook I used in my first course on what then was called mental retardation was George Baroff's *Mental Retardation: Nature, Cause, and Management* (1974). It was a well-written, engaging text covering what we now refer to as intellectual

6

disability. Back then, though, "mental retardation" was a *condition* linked closely to medical etiologies; fully half of the text was dedicated to medical aspects of the "condition" and how to manage it, medically and with regard to routines of daily living.

Think about the words I pulled from the earlier quotes about the purpose of P.L. 94-142: *treatment, prevention,* and *injury.* These are medical terms. As I was writing this chapter, I went back to issues of *Exceptional Children* from 1970 to 1979 and, other than the aforementioned discussions about the applicability of the medical model to special education *practices,* there was almost no discussion about how disability was understood.

That is because, as noted, there wasn't much that was in dispute about the idea that disability referred in some way to an internal pathology, disease, disorder, or impairment. Of course, a few people argued otherwise, but in general, and certainly among the general public, this was not a particularly controversial point. Certainly that was the case for what we now call intellectual disability. In the 8th revision of the *International Classification of Diseases* (ICD) issued by the World Health Organization (WHO), published in 1965 and in place at the time P.L. 94-142 was passed, mental retardation had its own code section (310–315), with each subsection reflecting "levels of impairment" (i.e., borderline, mild, moderate, severe, profound, unspecified). Right before that section, Code 308, were behavior disorders of childhood, which included autism and emotional and behavioral disorders. In 1978, the 9th revision of the ICD included, under mental disorders diagnosed in childhood, a variety of learning disabilities (dyslexia, aphasia, and dyscalculia).

The ICD is a medical classification system. It sets standards for the diagnosis and categorization of *diseases* and *disorders.* Eligibility for special education services has always been a two-part process, beginning with the diagnosis of the "disability." P.L. 94-142 stated that to be eligible for special education services, children had to be diagnosed "as being mentally retarded, hard of hearing, deaf, speech impaired, visually handicapped, seriously emotionally disturbed, orthopedically impaired or as having specific learning disabilities . . . who because of those impairments need special education and related services" [P.L. 94-142 Sec. 121a.5(a)].

It seems indisputable that disability in our society has been (and, I suggest, continues to be) understood as an extension of the medical model, independent of whether the medical model is implemented in special education practice. Disability, in any form, has been viewed through the lenses of the etiology that is the underlying cause of the "pathology," and people with those conditions have been viewed in some way, shape, or form as disordered.

The pathology orientation to understanding disability has not served people well, I believe. Certainly that is true for people with intellectual disability, who have been subject to legally sanctioned segregation, forced sterilization, institutionalization, and discrimination because, in essence, they are viewed as different from everyone else in society because of their "pathology." I have suggested in other books that what one learns by reading the history of intellectual disability is that when one is deemed to be different and (intellectually) inferior, it leads inevitably to maltreatment and discrimination.

Do you think that was true in the past, but not so much now? Consider that in the past decade, at least two major news stories have been reported in which people with developmental disabilities were enslaved by employers to engage in menial, often degrading labor at subminimum wages. Read *New York Times* reporter Dan Barry's book, *The Boys in the Bunkhouse: Servitude and Salvation in the Heartland* (2016), about men with intellectual disability who were forced to go to a turkey processing plant every day to gut turkeys in exchange for minimal food rations, substandard housing, and under $75 wages per month. One cannot do what was done to these men and simultaneously believe that they are valued, have dignity, and, fundamentally, are fully human.

How disability is understood by society also impacts the stigma associated with being labeled as having a disability, and not only for students with intellectual disability. The National Center for Learning Disabilities indicates that only one quarter of students with learning disabilities disclose their "disability" when they get to college. Why? The cost of doing so is greater, in their perception, than not doing so. Students say that they don't want to be thought of as not being *normal*, that they believe peers and professors will treat them differently if they disclose.

Andrew Batshaw, the son of physician Mark Batshaw, wrote about his learning disability in the first edition of his father's textbook on children with disabilities. I'll just let you read the quote from then-12-year-old Andrew and let you decide if these issues only pertain to some children with more severe disabilities:

> I remember when I almost failed first grade because I couldn't read. I would cry hour after hour because my mother would try to make me read. Now I love to read. I couldn't write in cursive but my mother helped me and now I can. I don't have as bad a learning disability as others. I am trying as hard as I can (I just hope it is enough). My worst nightmare is to go to a special school because I don't want to be treated differently. (Batshaw, 1989, p. xxxi)

PERSON–ENVIRONMENT FIT MODELS OF DISABILITY

The 1985 quote I used in the Introduction from Seymour Sarason stating that what we now refer to as intellectual disability is "never a thing or a characteristic of an individual, but rather a social invention stemming from time-bound societal values and ideology" (p. 233) should suggest that alternative ways to think about disability have existed for a long time.

I do understand that some people with disability and some scholars in the field question the utility of even talking about disability. People with "disabilities" are hardly a homogeneous group, and creating a single way to refer to them as a group is problematic. Even using the pronoun *them* in the previous sentence seems to suggest an otherness: an *us* versus *them* dichotomy. If there is one universal among people with disabilities that might justify efforts to think about how to discuss and define disability in more adaptive ways, it is that people with disabilities have experienced discrimination and marginalization as a function of what society perceives as their "differentness."

I think there are models on the horizon that don't necessitate labeling and categorization, and thus obviate the need for the notion of disability. But for now, as a starting point for that broader societal transformation, let's consider ways in which disability has been conceptualized that move us away from pathology and disease. The most visible and familiar of such conceptualizations have been forwarded by the WHO as alternatives to the ICD, discussed earlier in this chapter.

The first of these alternative classification systems was the *International Classification of Impairments, Disabilities, and Handicaps* (ICIDH), which was proposed by the WHO in 1980. As noted, prior WHO classification systems were intended to provide taxonomies of impairments, diseases, and disorders for diagnostic purposes. But, by the late 1970s the medical community had recognized that individual pathology models offered a too narrow perspective for effectively describing, understanding, and addressing the problems of people experiencing chronic or pervasive health issues, including disability. Thus the ICIDH was forwarded to provide a classification of the *consequences* of disease, injuries, and other disorders, and of the implications of such diseases, injuries, and disorders for the lives of the people experiencing them.

Clearly still situated in a medical context, the ICIDH (and the ICIDH-2, a revision issued in 1993) took the first steps toward externalizing disability; that is, situating disability somewhere external to the person (rather than an internal pathology). The WHO proposed three levels or types of classifications, all reflected in the title of the ICIDH. The first, *impairment*, referred to problems with body functions, structures, or anatomy. The second, *disability*, referred to problems in the person's activities resulting from impairment. The third, *handicap*, referred to problems in performing roles in society (WHO, 1980, p. 30).

As an attempt to provide a taxonomy of the consequences of impairments, disability, and handicaps, the ICIDH was a step in the right direction, but there were obvious problems, pointed out by people with disabilities and their families, advocates, researchers, and policymakers. For one, there was inadequate treatment of the important impact of context and environments—both physical and social—on disability. Also, like prior disease classifications, the ICIDH emphasized a unidirectional model: from impairments (i.e., disease, disorder) to disability (i.e., limitations in activities) to handicap (i.e., limitations in societal roles). The person, in other words, was still broken and was still the root cause of the problem that resulted in activity limitations and role restrictions. Add in the stigmatizing language (handicap) and the fact that disability was still isolated in a class of its own and apart from typical human functioning, and it is clear that while an important first step, the ICIDH did not go far enough.

In response to these criticisms, the WHO introduced the *International Classification of Functioning, Disability, and Health* (ICF) in 2001. The ICF situates disability as part of and not apart from typical human functioning and health. According to the WHO (2002):

> ICF is named as it is because its stress is on health and functioning, rather than on disability. Previously, disability began where health ended; once you were disabled, you were in a separate category. We want to get away from this kind of thinking. We want to make ICF a tool for measuring functioning in society, no matter what the reason for one's impairments. (p. 2)

The ICF defines *functioning* as an umbrella term for the interactions between a person's health (body functions, structures, anatomy) and contextual (physical and social) and personal factors that impact daily activities and participation. *Disability* is an umbrella term for "the negative aspects of the interaction between a person's health condition(s) and that individual's contextual factors" (WHO, 2001, p. 10).

The ICF is not a perfect system, but for the first time it provided a way to think about disability within the context of typical human functioning and health. A person could have a disability and still be healthy. Disability was a part of the continuum of typical human functioning.

Federal policy picked up on these changes in how disability was conceptualized. The Rehabilitation Act of 1992 stated:

> Disability is a natural part of the human experience and in no way diminishes the rights of individuals to live independently, enjoy self-determination, make choices, contribute to society, pursue meaningful careers and enjoy full inclusion and integration in the economic, political, social, cultural and educational mainstream of American society. [Rehabilitation Act Amendments of 1992, Sec. 2 (a)(3)(A–F)]

That language was incorporated into the IDEA reauthorization of 1997 and the Developmental Disabilities Assistance and Bill of Rights Act of 2000. In 1992, the ICIDH was the basis for a substantial revision of the terminology and classification manual of the then-named American Association on Mental Retardation (now the American Association on Intellectual and Developmental Disabilities, or AAIDD). In defining the construct "mental retardation," the manual made the following statement:

> Mental retardation is not something you have, like blue eyes or a bad heart. Nor is it something you are, like being short or thin. Mental retardation refers to a particular state of functioning that begins in childhood and in which limitations in intelligence coexist with related limitations in adaptive skill. As a statement about functioning, it describes the "fit" between the capabilities of the individual and the structure and expectations of the individual's personal and social environment. (Lukasson et al., 1992, p. 9)

Since the 1992 edition of the manual, the AAIDD has changed the term used to describe this "state of functioning" to intellectual disability. Some of you may well be familiar with the changes in conceptualization associated with disability, but even if this is familiar territory, let me pose a question. If we have embraced these ways of thinking about disability, why do we still say that a person "has" intellectual disability or a physical disability or autism? I'm going to suggest it is because we still cling to the vestiges of conceptualizations of disability as disorder or pathology—as a problem within the person. So, one sense of going "beyond disability" reflects our need to go "beyond pathology."

These models of disability have gone by a variety of names. The most awkward to pronounce is biopsychosocial models, which refers to the biological, psychological, and social components of understanding disability. The easier-to-digest and more widely used term is social–ecological models. I have always preferred the notion of person–environment fit models, because this more clearly communicates that disability lies only in the gap between a person's capacities and the demands of the environment.

I also prefer the term *person–environment fit* because the term translates more readily to the design of interventions for all learners. Think about some of the innovative practices in the past decade or so, such as, for example, positive behavior supports (PBS). PBS is perhaps the most successfully scaled-up intervention to emerge from our field. How is PBS best defined? Ted Carr and colleagues (1999) argued that at its heart PBS is "an approach for dealing with problem behavior that focuses on the remediation of deficient contexts" (p. 15). I think most people think about PBS as an approach to remediate deficient behavior. But that's the disability-as-pathology influence coming into play again. Think instead about PBS within a person–environment fit model. We seek to improve personal capacity and functioning and to modify the demands of the environment and provide supports that make problem behavior unnecessary for the person.

Or, consider another widely discussed innovation, Universal Design for Learning (UDL). We'll talk more about technology and UDL subsequently, but I'll just point out that UDL involves changes to the way in which learning materials and content are presented or represented and the ways in which students respond. If a child cannot read, that child will not benefit from content that is provided only in a print book. Change the format to a digital talking book, and we can harness text-to-speech capacities of the technology to provide access to that content and increase the probability of learning. UDL involves modifications to the context, where the context refers to learning materials, just as stipulated by person–environment fit models.

There are more examples that we'll leave for consideration in subsequent chapters. Person–environment fit models of disability provide powerful ways to think about disability and to enable young people to be successful, independent of any diagnosis, label, or category. What is important is what the child can do, what we can do to the context to support success, and what supports we can put in place to narrow the gap between a person's capacities and the demands of the environment. And, equally powerfully, person–environment fit models are inherently strengths-based.

STRENGTHS-BASED APPROACHES TO DISABILITY

In 2011, I was asked by Oxford University Press to edit a new handbook for their Handbooks in Psychology series. The resulting text, *The Oxford Handbook of Positive Psychology and Disability* (Wehmeyer, 2013), was, as far as I'm aware, the first comprehensive treatment of the application of positive psychological constructs to the disability context.

Think for a minute about what it means to pair positive psychology with disability. Consider how positive psychology has been defined. Martin Seligman and Mihaly Csikszentmihalyi (2000), two of the founders and most influential scholars in the field, said this about the discipline:

> Positive psychology is, at the individual level, about positive individual traits: the capacity for love and vocation, courage, interpersonal skill, aesthetic sensibility, perseverance, forgiveness, originality, future mindedness, spirituality, high talent, and wisdom. (p. 5)

Chris Peterson (2009), who studied under Seligman and pioneered research in character strengths, defined positive psychology in his Foreword to the 2nd edition of *The Oxford Handbook of Positive Psychology* as:

> The "scientific" study of what makes life most worth living. It is a call for psychological science and practice to be as concerned with strength as with weakness: as interested in building the best things in life as in repairing the worst; and as concerned with making the lives of normal people fulfilling as with healing pathology. (p. xxiii)

The Table of Contents to that 2nd edition of *The Oxford Handbook of Positive Psychology* (Snyder & Lopez, 2009) reflects the field's focus on positive attributes. Topics include happiness, subjective well-being, optimism, faith and religiosity, self-determination, creativity, giftedness, positive youth development, positive emotions, character strengths, resilience, aging well, positive affectivity, mindfulness, problem-solving appraisal, compassion, empathy and altruism, gratitude, humility, toughness, positive schools, positive workplaces, spirituality, and more.

Returning to my task in 2011 to edit a handbook on positive psychology and disability, until nearly that time, we, as a field, simply did not have a language to talk about disability in terms of optimal human functioning and well-being, much less heed Peterson's call for a psychology of strengths versus weaknesses.

But person–environment fit models provide a way of conceptualizing disability that lets us talk about strengths-based approaches to disability and compels us to design interventions that focus on strengths rather than weaknesses, including positive youth development tasks, creativity, problem-solving capacity, self-determination, and more. Within such a strengths-based approach, we begin with what it is that students are good at, their interests and preferences, and their abilities and capacities. We look at how to change or modify the context in ways that further support successful functioning, and we identify supports that further bridge the gap between what a student can do and what the context or environment demands.

Let's take resilience as an example of how these changes can play out. Most people are familiar with the idea of resilience as a visible construct in positive psychology. It is the idea that some people have some qualities or characteristics that enable them to overcome hardships to succeed or to bounce back from difficulties. Historically, resilience has been understood as a trait of a person. A person is or isn't resilient, depending on what they do or don't do or what qualities or characteristics they have or don't have.

When I first began looking at issues pertaining to self-determination as they applied to disability, I thought that the overlap between resilience and self-determination might provide some assistance in understanding how to promote the self-determination of students with disabilities. Unfortunately, at that time most conceptualizations of resilience (as a personal trait) included the criteria that the person have average or above-average intelligence. Of course, that excluded any person with intellectual disability as being resilient. That struck me as just wrong, since I knew a lot of people with intellectual disability who had overcome barriers and hurdles in the form of segregation and discrimination to live the lives they wanted. If they were not resilient, I thought, then nobody was.

Fast forward to today. In her book *Resilience Begins with Beliefs: Building on Student Strengths for Success in School* (2014), Sara Truebridge describes how the shift from understanding resilience as a trait to that of a process opens the door for presuming that all students have the capacity for resilience. Resilience is the "dynamic and negotiated process within individuals (internal) and between individuals and their environments (external) for the resources and supports to adapt and define themselves as healthy amid adversity, threat, trauma and/or everyday stress" (p. xx).

The "internal" elements of resilience are not innate, inborn characteristics of people, but involve "tapping into one's personal strengths, attributes, past experiences" (p. 12). The major developmental supports and opportunities that nourish resilience are caring relationships, high expectations, and opportunities to participate and contribute. Resilience involves adaptation to adversity, and adaptation is critical to self-determined learning and self-determination, as we'll discuss in Chapter 8. And guess what? One of the most immediate steps we can take to create schools that provide opportunities to promote resilience is to move from a "deficit-based perspective to a strengths-based perspective" (p. 54). Person–environment fit models provide a strengths-based perspective that will enable us to talk about nourishing the capacity of children with disabilities to become resilient.

BEYOND DISABILITY IN THE EDUCATION OF ALL LEARNERS

I really do not see any road forward that has us hanging on to historical conceptualizations of disability. We have, I would argue, gone as far as we can go to achieve the educational outcomes we desire, if we understand disability within a medical model. Let me be clear that I'm not saying that there is no value to understanding the underlying neurological, physical, or anatomical reasons that disability manifests. There is value to knowing that children with Down syndrome mature in their motor skills at a delayed rate or to understanding the areas of the brain involved with dyslexia. Within the ICF, the limitations of body function, structure, or anatomy are not excluded; they're just not given sole primacy in determining outcomes.

And, within person–environment fit models of disability, if we can successfully bridge the gap between a person's capacities and the demands of the environment (by enhancing capacity, modifying the environment, or providing supports) so that the person is able to function successfully, disability itself becomes irrelevant. It takes us beyond disability as something we spend much time worrying about.

CHAPTER 2

Beyond Programs

Supports and Support Needs

I've used the term *supports* a number of times, and you'll see the term appended to the name of innovative practices—positive behavior *supports* and multi-tiered systems of *supports*, to name just two. It's important that we understand clearly what we mean by supports, because identifying supports to operationalize a personalizable education for learners with disabilities is, in my mind, how we move beyond a "program" mentality in the education of learners with disabilities.

PROGRAMS AND SERVICES

What do I mean by "move beyond a program mentality"? Of course, in 1975, P.L. 94-142 was focused on establishing "appropriate educational programs" for students with "handicaps." In a 1977 article about the then-upcoming (in 1978) full implementation of P.L. 94-142, Alan Abeson (who, like Fred Weintraub, was in the Governmental Relations Department at CEC and helped craft the language in the law) said this:

> The first criteria [*sic*] [discussing eligibility] is whether the child has one or more of the disabilities listed in the definition. The second is whether the child requires special education and related services. Not all children who have disability require special education, many can and should attend school without any program modification. (Abeson & Zettel, 1977, p. 124)

Education as a "program" is at the heart of P.L. 94-142; individualized education programs were intended to modify educational programs that were not working for some students with disabilities. The definitions in P.L. 94-142 went to great lengths to distinguish a program, referring to what would be provided to the child, versus a plan, which implied guidelines "from which a program must subsequently be developed" (Abeson & Zettel, 1977, p. 124). Intended or not, the notion of a program quickly became conflated with ideas of homogeneous grouping.

I don't think the framers of P.L. 94-142 intended to promulgate the establishment of separate programs; otherwise the language pertaining to least restrictive environment would not be in the Act. I had the privilege of working for Alan Abeson in the 1990s at the headquarters of The Arc, the national advocacy organization for families and people with intellectual and developmental disabilities, when he was executive director, and he was as frustrated with the lack of progress in educating students with disabilities in general education settings as anyone else. I just think that the zeitgeist of the 1970s was that disability as a pathology led logically to children with disabilities being served in programs to meet their supposedly unique medical, educational, communication, and social needs. Traditional conceptualizations of disability that emphasized deficits, diagnosis, and categorization inevitably resulted in the creation of programs that met the supposedly unique needs of people within those rather broad categories.

In one of my teaching assignments in the early 1980s, I was the "special education" teacher for a school district's "severely and profoundly handicapped" (SPH) class for adolescents (broadly defined as 12–21 years of age!). This class was located in a separate campus building. It was a relatively small, square building located in proximity to an elementary school. The building housed the district's adolescent SPH class, two trainable "mentally handicapped" (TMH) classes, one class for adolescents with emotional and behavioral disorders who had been expelled from their neighborhood school, and one more class for five young men with intellectual disability who also were labeled as having emotional and behavioral disorders. Sadly enough, each morning these five young men traveled from the group home in which all of them lived to this segregated classroom in a separate campus building, thus keeping them pretty much under 24-hour-a-day surveillance.

Students who were identified for the SPH and TMH categories were placed in those respective classes as a function of their diagnosis and their level of intellectual functioning, as determined by an intelligence test. They were grouped together under the assumption that as a result of their intellectual functioning or, in some cases for students in my class, intellectual functioning and physical, sensory, or medical complications, the students would need the same curriculum, the same types of instruction, the same types of equipment and related services, and so forth.

Mind you, IDEA has always required that students receiving special education services be educated with their nondisabled peers, with needed supplementary aids and services, unless that proved not to be feasible. But, certainly none of the students in my self-contained class had ever spent even an hour in a general education classroom, and I can't think of a single student with more extensive support needs that I've known or worked with over the years who arrived in the self-contained setting by route of failed efforts to be educated in a general education classroom.

Instead, because of the ways in which disability has been understood and because of the historical models of how people with disabilities were treated (in separate places, in homogeneously grouped segregated settings), this was just the way things were done when P.L. 94-142 came into being. Students were evaluated, labeled, and then placed into a "program" that supposedly best fit their needs and where the district could concentrate resources to theoretically serve them better. Opponents of "inclusion" point to the purported lack of evidence to support inclusion. What nobody mentions is that de facto segregation occurred without a shred of evidence that it was the best way to proceed. It was simply what had been done for the preceding decades, and so we did it.

But, anyway, back to my early teaching experience. The building also housed a school psychologist, a sheltered workshop, and a simulated kitchen/laundry/bedroom to teach daily living skills. Turns out, it had been built with federal funds made available to schools and universities in the early 1960s from the John F. Kennedy administration's push to move people with intellectual disability into their communities (and out of institutions).

When it was established in 1962, and certainly in 1975 when P.L. 94-142 was implemented, this "program" was state of the art. It was the best that was imaginable. Even when I taught there in the early 1980s, the building was still pretty nice (and had some dedicated, caring people teaching and working there, I should add). Students, it was argued, could learn the skills they needed in order to be more independent. They could learn skills that might help them get sheltered work when they graduated. There were speech therapists and occupational therapists and physical therapists and psychologists and special education teachers and para-educators—a whole army of highly trained professionals to prepare them for life.

Of course, by 1984 when I arrived on the scene, there were cracks in the foundation of this approach (if not the actual building itself, which I suspect is still in use in the district). Certainly, it didn't work for any of the students I spent 4 years teaching. None of them made it to the sheltered workshop. All, as far as I know, ended up living at home with their parents, some of them going to day habilitation programs akin to babysitting. I believe my students were better off having had access to education, and I believe their parents thought so as well. But it was the depressingly poor outcomes associated with that experience for those students that compelled me to get my doctorate and see whether there wasn't some better way to go about this whole enterprise.

And it's not just placement decisions that fall into the "program" mentality trap. How many times have you seen a district create a program as a means to implement an innovation? These are pilot efforts that only some students get access to. The most egregious of these are district "inclusion programs" that exclude some students based upon of the severity of their impairments.

The fact is that people within similar deficits-oriented IQ bands or within particular disorder typologies (e.g., Down syndrome, cerebral palsy, dyslexia, ADHD, etc.) are as different from one another as they are similar.

Programs that are designed to meet the needs of homogeneously grouped learners have not, in fact, shown that they meet these needs and too often ignore the highly unique needs of learners.

Creating programs hasn't really worked. I feel much the same when I hear people talking about services. Of course, the IDEA language is also replete with "service" terms—special education services, related services, supplementary aids and services, transition services, early intervention services, assistive technology services, and so forth. A service is an activity or commodity or the performance of a duty needed by someone. But, too often when I hear the term *services* applied to a disability context, it really means that this or that program is an option; that one may or may not qualify for that program or service; and that there is a one-size-fits-all element to the provision of services.

Perhaps I protest too much. But, while special education has always been defined in IDEA as specially designed instruction, it is widely interpreted to mean a program or service-delivery model: a program students go to or attend to get the education they need because of their deficits or pathology. Go ahead, google "special education program" and check the news sources and see how many times the news report refers to students attending, entering, or being placed in a special education program. It's a place students go, a program they attend to get the services they supposedly need.

Beyond Compliance. Before I leave the topic of programs, let me add another "beyond" that I think is closely associated with a program focus: We need to go beyond a compliance mentality if we are to really educate all children. Catherine Kramarczuk Voulgarides has written a compelling book titled *Does Compliance Matter in Special Education? IDEA and the Hidden Inequities of Practice* (Voulgarides, 2018). The focus of Voulgarides's analysis of the impacts of a compliance focus in special education is on racial disproportionality in special education. We've known for some time that students from some racial and ethnic populations are identified to receive special education at higher rates than students from other racial and ethnic groups and also to be placed in more restrictive environments at higher rates.

The U.S. Department of Education tracks this using a risk ratio statistic, which is calculated as a ratio of children in a particular racial/ethnic group as a function of all children receiving special education. A risk ratio of 1.0 means that children in that racial/ethnic category are equally likely to receive special education services as all other racial/ethnic groups. A risk ratio of 2.0 means that children in that racial/ethnic category are twice as likely to receive special education services as are all other racial/ethnic groups.

In the *39th Annual Report to Congress on the Implementation of the IDEA* (U.S. Department of Education, 2018), the Office of Special Education Programs indicates that for children ages 6 through 21, American

Indian or Alaska Native children have a risk ratio of 1.7, Black or African American children have a risk ratio of 1.4, and Native Hawaiian or Other Pacific Islander children have a risk ratio of 1.5. White (0.9) and Asian (0.5) children were the only groups with risk ratios under 1.0, indicating they are less likely than all other racial/ethnic groups to receive special education services.

If you look at the risk ratio for children 6 to 21 within racial/ethnic groups by disability category, African American children are twice as likely as all other racial/ethnic groups to be categorized as having an emotional or behavioral disorder and more than twice as likely (risk ratio 2.2) to be identified as having intellectual disability. American Indian or Alaska Native children also had high risk ratios for being labeled as having intellectual disability (1.6) or emotional or behavioral disorder (1.7), as did Native Hawaiian or Other Pacific Island children (1.7, 1.3 respectively).

Voulgarides's analysis focused on attempts to address these ongoing racial disparities in the 2004 reauthorization of IDEA. In that reauthorization, the Office of Special Education Programs developed 20 "State Performance Plan indicators," and (from the OSEP IDEA website at sites.ed.gov/idea/spp-apr/) required states to submit reports of targets set (in the state performance plan) on these 20 indicators of "child and family outcomes and other indicators that measure compliance with the requirements of the IDEA."

Three such indicators addressed disproportionality in special education, specific disability categories, and in suspensions of students of color. There are multiple reasons that this compliance focus has not reduced racial disproportionality. For one, Voulgarides cited research showing that states vary in the definition they set for what determines overrepresentation, with some using the 2.0 relative risk ratio, and others using as high as 4.0. For another, the use of a "deficits framework" (discussed in Chapter 1), as Voulgarides worded it, "places the responsibility of learning on individual bodies and does not sufficiently question how social structures, norms, and systems contribute to persistent inequalities in education" (p. 4).

The data collected for these indicators reflect heavily on the issue of compliance. For example, for Indicator 4, which focuses on issues pertaining to suspensions of children of color, data are collected by reviewing student records for the presence of positive behavior supports, reviewing IEPs for the presence of behavioral supports and interventions, reviewing behavior intervention plans, and so forth. Voulgarides provided an example of an all-too-familiar outcome from a focus on compliance: She attended a professional development meeting in one district in which almost all of 3 hours was spent teaching the district's psychologists how to correctly fill out a section of the IEP to follow new procedural mandates from the state. She noted that, during this meeting, "nearly 90 minutes of heated discussion ensued between the psychologists and the administrative team about locating where a date and signature should be on an IEP" (p. 19).

Voulgarides argues compellingly that not only does the deficits-focused, compliance-oriented nature of special education not remedy the issue of disproportionality, such a focus in fact exacerbates the problem. The "logic of compliance . . . undermines equity, because when educators work in schools and districts that are found to be disproportionate, yet can show compliance with IDEA, it implies that educators are faithfully applying the law and adhering to the principles of equal educational opportunity and access" (p. 84).

We'll return to these issues of compliance versus meaningful outcomes in a subsequent chapter on going beyond individualization and "de minimus" education (Chapter 5), but I believe that the points made by Voulgarides pertaining to the negative impact of a compliance mentality on the serious problem of racial disproportionality can be applied to most of the areas in IDEA that the performance indicators are supposed to remedy. Think about this when, in Chapter 8, we discuss the employment outcomes for young people with disabilities. Indicator 13 addresses compliance with transition-related goals in IDEA by requiring districts and states to collect data on activities such as the presence of goals on the IEP, the use of age-appropriate assessments, and whether the student was invited to the IEP meeting. Despite the fact that I do understand the logic of the attempt to regulate compliance with these activities as a means to influence outcomes like disproportionality or transition to adulthood, the relationship between compliance and meaningful outcomes seems tenuous, at best. A 2013 study of the relationship between Indicator 13 compliance and more positive postsecondary outcomes for youth with disabilities found some relationship between compliance with Indicator 13 and completion of a college semester and enrollment in noncollege training programs, but the effect sizes were very small and there was no evidence of impacts of compliance on rates of college completion or postsecondary employment (Erickson, Noonan, Brussow, & Gilpin, 2014).

The suggestions that Voulgarides makes with regard to going beyond compliance to address the important issue of racial disproportionality are, I think, consistent with many of the big ideas I've tried to highlight in this book. We begin by going beyond disability and beyond programs and we create learning communities that emphasize that all children can learn and that create meaningful opportunities for all students. That is what the next section introduces.

DEEP LEARNING AND A WORLD-CLASS EDUCATION

The important question we must ask ourselves is whether this is the model we want to use as we move further into the 21st century. Has it served children with disabilities well? Now is as good a time as any to think a bit about a topic we'll consider in greater depth in a later chapter: What will students need to be successful in the next decades and how should we provide education to prepare students for that future?

Everything I read about what learners need to be prepared to do in the next several decades—what my colleague Yong Zhao (2012) frames as being a world-class learner—refers to student autonomy in and ownership of learning, the importance of education harnessing student curiosity and motivation, product-oriented learning and entrepreneurship, engaging the world, and "deep learning" (Fullan, Quinn, & McEachen, 2018). Michael Fullan and colleagues define deep learning as "valuable learning that *sticks*—it situates the learner as someone who acts upon the world (usually with others) thereby transforming her- or himself *and* the world itself" (p. xvii, emphasis in original).

Deep learning "increases student engagement in the learning through personalization and ownership" and "connects students to the 'real world,' which is often more reflective of their own reality and cultural identity" (Fullan et al., 2018, p. 9). A world-class education, according to Zhao (2012), is characterized by student voice in school governance and environment, student choice in a broad and flexible curriculum, and a strengths-based focus on student uniqueness and curiosity.

I don't see a program or services paradigm getting us to where we need to be if these are the characteristics of learning and schools in the future. Instead, we need to think about providing supports that enable young people to bridge the gap between what they can do and what they want to do; indeed, what they need to do if they are to be successful in the coming decades.

SUPPORTS AND SUPPORT NEEDS

So, back to my earlier point of needing to understand what, exactly, we mean by supports. The shift from deficits-based models of disability to person–environment fit models brought about a broader and more nuanced discussion of supports. Some of the work I have been involved with (with many colleagues) involves how we understand and measure supports. Why measure? It remains the case, for good or bad, that what we measure becomes what we focus on. Our efforts to understand disability based upon person–environment fit models of disability needed some way to quantify the notion of supports.

In that work, we defined supports as "resources and strategies that aim to promote the development, education, interests, and personal well-being of a person and that enhance individual functioning" (Luckasson et al., 2002, p. 151). I think, though, that all of us involved in this enterprise of defining and operationalizing measures of support would sheepishly admit that this definition basically says that supports are, really, anything that enables someone to function successfully, participate in society, pursue meaningful goals, and live a self-determined life.

We all use supports. I was in Tokyo, Japan, a few years ago, and the meeting I was to attend on a university campus was a half-hour walk from the hotel where I was staying. I studied the map of the local vicinity and confidently headed along the route I had identified, and promptly was lost in a maze of narrow streets identified only by signage with Japanese language characters. I weighed my options and proceeded to turn on the cellular functions of my smartphone, deciding that paying the exorbitant international fees was preferable to wandering about Tokyo for a day. The blinking blue dot on the maps app on my phone located me, and within a few seconds I was back on track and made my meeting with no difficulty.

Supports are more than technology, though. Supports are people: friends, family, co-workers, neighbors, professionals—anyone whom we can rely on or utilize to support or enable us to get where we want to go. Supports include money, libraries, public transportation, financial services, ramps and modifications, mobility devices, accommodations, adaptations, and, indeed, specially designed instruction. Education is a powerful support; it enhances one's capacity to act on one's environment and achieve goals. Supplementary aids and services, as specified in IDEA, are forms of supports: the roles of special educators and para-educators, the use of educational and assistive technology, modifications to tests and instructional activities. Universal Design for Learning is a way to talk about supports that promote learning: digital talking books that provide cognitive access, text-to-speech devices, translation technology. The laptop computer I'm using to type this manuscript is a support. I suppose the coffee I'm drinking this morning is another form of support!

There are some qualifications for what is or is not a support. Supports definitionally and theoretically are situated in the notions of personal well-being and individual functioning. The latter is linked to notions in the ICF pertaining to functioning as an umbrella term for typical functioning, full participation, and active engagement in life. Supports promote functioning and participation in the community. Further, they promote personal well-being. Supports pertain to enabling people to live real lives in their communities.

Supports are personal. Sure, some supports have wide applicability to support all people. My smartphone map app is one such universal support. But I don't need access to electronic Braille or haven't needed a 3D printer to print a customized hand grip cup holder. Some people's needed supports include such specialized items. Line 10 people up in a row who all test the same on an IQ test, and you're going to find 10 unique profiles of needed supports. And that applies in whatever part of the bell curve one's IQ happens to fall.

Supports are personal and it is through supports, in part, that we can create a personalizable education, about which I'll talk more in a subsequent chapter. Before turning attention to personalizable education, however, I want to talk just a bit about where our work in creating a measure of supports has taken us. If the notion of supports encompasses virtually anything at all that might result in enhanced functioning and improved personal well-being, how in the world does one measure it? One cannot measure supports by counting all of the supports that are available or used by a person.

Let me back up just a bit, though, and talk about our intentions in creating a measure of supports. In the field of intellectual disability and, I would argue, throughout special education, measures quantify primarily personal characteristics, qualities, knowledge, skills, or abilities. Operationalizing a person–environment fit model of disability, however, would focus not on measuring the personal capacity of the individual, but instead on measuring the supports inherent in bridging the gap between personal capacity and the demands of the environment.

Our solution to the measurement dilemma was to create a measure of the type, duration, and intensity of supports a person would need in order to successfully function in typical contexts and environments. The resulting product, the Supports Intensity Scale (Thompson et al., 2004), measures the intensity of a person's support needs. Support needs are defined as "the pattern and intensity of supports necessary for a person to participate in activities linked to normative human functioning" (Thompson et al., 2009, p. 135). Higher levels of support needs in areas measured suggest that more or more-intense supports are needed for the person to be successful in that context. This is not a measure of personal competence; it is a measure of the intensity of a person's support needs across multiple typical contexts.

We recently published the Supports Intensity Scale—Children's Version (SIS-C) (Thompson et al., 2016). The SIS-C provides a standardized measure of the support needs of children ages 5 to 16 (the adult version provides similar information for adolescents and adults 16 years of age and older). The measure looks at intensity, type, and frequency of needed supports in the domains of home living activities, community and neighborhood activities, school participation activities, school learning activities, health and safety activities, social activities, and advocacy activities.

We developed the SIS-A and the SIS-C to measure the support needs of children, youth, and adults with intellectual disability because the need for extraordinary supports is one feature of the state of functioning we refer to as intellectual disability. But the idea behind this measure is one that has potential applicability for all learners: How can we use assessment to identify where students need additional supports to master content, learn material, and assume greater autonomy and ownership over learning, independent of why the student needs such supports?

BEYOND PROGRAMS IN THE EDUCATION OF ALL LEARNERS

How might a shift to a supports paradigm influence the education of learners with disabilities and, indeed, all learners? For one thing, theoretically we might be able to eliminate the need for disability diagnosis and classification as a prerequisite for getting educational supports that are personalized to each student's needs. It is not only children with disabilities who are struggling in a one-size-fits-all, standardized curriculum, high-stakes testing model. I understand that resources are limited and that one purpose of diagnosis and classification is to ensure that these scarce resources get to students who need them most. Or, at least I understand that is the intent. But, how many resources are used to determine eligibility for special education services? How many resources are used to bus children to a special program? How many resources are used to maintain wholly separate classrooms?

What if we used those resources to provide personalized supports to all children who need them? I think that is what schoolwide applications like multi-tiered systems of supports have the promise to do. We'll come back to those innovations later. What if the silos of federally funded programs, such as programs for English language learners, special education programs, or Title I programs for children from low-income families, were used to provide supports for children who were not succeeding under typical education conditions? Children served in all of these programs experience a gap between what they currently know or can do and what is needed for them to be successful in their lives. What if we went "beyond programs" to harness the power of deep learning and a world-class education, and provided supports that narrowed that gap for all learners?

CHAPTER 3

Beyond Individualization

Personalizable Education

We, as a field, talk a lot about the importance of individualization. We talk about individualized education programs and about individualizing instruction. Individualization was, presumably, at the heart of P.L. 94-142. Looking back to 1977:

> To deal with the past problems of inappropriate educational services being provided to children who have handicaps, the Congress included as a major component of P.L. 94-142 a requirement that each child be provided with a written individualized education program known as the IEP. The IEP required for each handicapped child is the central building block to understanding and effectively complying with the Act. (Abeson & Zettel, 1977, p. 123)

I say "presumably" because in hindsight it seems pretty clear that the zeitgeist of disability as pathology and of education as programs (and for many students for much of that time, segregated programs) that was in place in the mid-1970s would not have resulted in true individualization. I once reviewed a stack of about 150 IEPs for adolescents with intellectual disability from a large school district. I was reviewing them to see whether these students, all of whom were classified as having "moderate mental retardation," had goals pertaining to self-determination. To my dismay, not only did they not have any goals pertaining to self-determination, but, in fact, with the exception of the demographic information, the IEPs were identical. Not just similar. They were exactly the same. Why? Someone obviously believed that if a student had an IQ score between 40 and 55, then that student would need the exact same thing every other student in the district within that IQ range would need.

Not only are IEPs not very individualized, but our system is set up to group learners homogeneously in programs based upon deficits, so in reality instruction is more likely to be impacted by those programs, and by classifications resulting from assessments of personal incompetence, than to be truly individualized. The advent of computer-based IEPs has exacerbated what was already an issue: Goals and learning objectives are not highly individualized. For the vast majority of students with disabilities, the IEP still describes a substantially separate curriculum and not the individualized supports, supplementary aids and services, and specially designed instruction needed for a learner to be involved with and progress in the general education curriculum.

If we're to meet 21st-century demands for educating students with disabilities, we're going to need to go "beyond individualization," as it too often is practiced currently. I would argue that this was the message sent by the U.S. Supreme Court in the 2017 *Endrew F. v. Douglas County School District* ruling, which interpreted an *appropriate education* as implying that each student receiving IDEA services has a right to an *appropriately ambitious* educational program. The question becomes, what is an "appropriately ambitious" education in 2020 and beyond? I touched on this in the previous chapter when talking about deep learning and a world-class education. So let's think about what a 21st-century education should look like for any student.

A 21ST-CENTURY EDUCATION

The Partnership for 21st Century Skills (P21, now the Partnership for 21st Century Learning) was established just after the turn of the century as an initiative of the U.S. Department of Education; teacher organizations such as the National Education Association (NEA); national associations that establish standards in the areas of music, science, social studies, math, geography, and English and foreign languages; and thought leaders and stakeholders in the education, business, and policy communities. A report from the NEA (2016) frames the issue P21 was founded to address:

> America's system of education was built for an economy and a society that no longer exists. In the manufacturing and agrarian economies that existed 50 years ago, it was enough to master the "Three Rs" (reading, writing, and arithmetic). In the modern "flat world," the "Three Rs" simply aren't enough. If today's students want to compete in this global society, however, they must also be proficient communicators, creators, critical thinkers, and collaborators (the "Four Cs"). (p. 5)

The "Four Cs" have become a widely used framework to discuss 21st-century skills. These skills appear in virtually all taxonomies of 21st-century education, so let's examine why each of these is considered critical as we think about what a 21st-century education should look like for students with (and without) disabilities.

Collaboration

You probably don't need to be convinced that the world is more connected than at any other time in history. In my own work, I collaborate with colleagues in Australia and Chile using videoconferencing; write papers with colleagues from Spain, Taiwan, South Korea, and Italy using Dropbox; review papers from research teams in Poland or Taiwan using Internet-based editorial software; and answer doctoral student inquiries from around the world using email. And, my younger colleagues far exceed my rudimentary use of technology to be productive! Collaboration has always been important, but in the 21st-century world, it is critical. The NEA report stated it like this:

> Collaboration is essential in our classrooms because it is inherent in the nature of how work is accomplished in our civic and workforce lives. Fifty years ago, much work was accomplished by individuals working alone, but not today. Much of all significant work is accomplished in teams, and in many cases, global teams. (p. 19)

Research synthesized by the P21 consortia concluded that collaboration skills—including interpersonal communication, conflict resolution, and task management skills—are critical for more effective school and work performance and are highly valued by employers (Plucker, Kennedy, & Dilley, 2017).

Communication

Like collaboration, communication as the second "C" seems uncontroversial. Employers want employees with effective communication skills; collaboration, critical thinking, and creativity require effective communication skills; and communication skills are highly related to student academic success (Dilley, Fishlock, & Plucker, 2017). The NEA report again puts it succinctly:

> Expressing thoughts clearly, crisply articulating opinions, communicating coherent instructions, motivating others through powerful speech—these skills have always been valued in the workplace and in public life. But in the 21st century, these skills have been transformed and are even more important today. (p. 13)

Critical Thinking

It is evident that 21st-century citizens will need to exercise judgment, solve problems, consider alternatives, weigh information, and make decisions about everything from their health to the environment to the world of work. One need only consider the issue of climate change to see how limitations in such skills have paralyzed potentially critical action. A consensus definition of critical thinking categorized it in two dimensions: (1) cognitive skills, which are needed to interpret, analyze, infer, explain, and self-regulate action, and (2) dispositional elements that are needed for the energization of the cognitive dimensions: inquisitiveness, curiosity, flexibility, persistence, and orderliness, among others (Dilley, Kaufman, Kennedy, & Plucker, 2017).

Creativity

None of the "Four Cs" are really new to education. But issues pertaining to creativity, innovation, and entrepreneurship have risen to the top of lists that describe what young people need to be able to do to be successful in the 21st century. The NEA guide to preparing 21st-century students for a global society quotes multiple visionaries who attest to this: author Daniel Pink, who pointed out that "the future belongs to a very different kind of person with a very different kind of mind—creators and empathizers, pattern recognizers and meaning makers"; British education futurist Sir Kenneth Robinson, who stated that "creativity is as important in education as literacy and we should treat it with the same status"; and psychologist Robert Sternberg, who noted that "successful individuals are those who have creative skills, to produce a vision for how they intend to make the world a better place for everyone; analytical intellectual skills, to assess their vision and those of others; practical intellectual skills, to carry out their vision and persuade people of its value; and wisdom, to ensure that their vision is not a selfish one" (cited in NEA, 2016, p. 24).

If communication, collaboration, critical thinking, and creativity are the skills that all young people need to succeed in 2020 and beyond, I feel pretty certain that we had better figure out how we provide students with disabilities the supports that will prepare them with the "Four Cs," or they will be left behind. And, let's be honest here, a lot of people would look at that list and presume that young people with disabilities will not be able to acquire the skills needed in order to collaborate productively, communicate effectively, think critically, and act creatively.

I like to tell audiences to whom I'm speaking that I have been in this field long enough to have familiarized myself with the research literature over 5 decades, beginning in the 1970s and up through today, and that I have concluded from that literature that there is only one universal truth that ties these decades of knowledge together. That truth is that if we look at what was expected of people with disabilities in any given decade, they far exceeded those expectations in the following decade. What we have expected of people with disabilities has always been wrong. And, it will be again. What people with disabilities achieve is less about their characteristics and more about opportunity, expectations, and supports.

So, I don't count myself among those who believe that young people with disabilities cannot learn to collaborate, communicate effectively, think critically, and act creatively, nor, I suspect, do you if you are reading this. We will, however, have to raise the bar substantially if we are to provide the opportunities, expectations, and supports that will enable young people to succeed in the 21st century. One does not learn to collaborate and communicate in segregated, separate settings. One does not learn to think critically and creatively when instruction is based upon diagnoses and labels. To provide an education that enables young people with disabilities to acquire 21st-century skills, we need to go beyond individualization to provide a personalizable education.

GOING FOR GREAT

I have learned to embrace the idea of students with disabilities being successful 21st-century learners because of my own collaborations and communication with a colleague, Yong Zhao, and his creativity and critical thinking about 21st-century learning. Our own "Four Cs," if you will.

Yong's work and life embody the rich possibilities of globalization, technology, creativity, and entrepreneurship. Born and raised in a rural farming village in southwest China, in *Reach for Greatness: Personalizable Education for All Children* (2018), Yong described his success not in terms of his skills and abilities, but as due to the fact that "no one tried to fix my deficits" (p. 4). That he is successful is self-evident. In addition to attaining the highest levels in academia, he is one of the most visible thought leaders in 21st-century education, appearing regularly on lists of the most influential education scholars in publications like *Education Week*.

Yong's trajectory to thought leader in education was not as evident when he was a young boy back in China:

> I was born in a Chinese village . . . destined to become a farmer like everyone else. But from a very early age, I discovered that I was not cut out to be a successful farmer. I was physically smaller and weaker than other boys. I could not drive water buffalos or climb trees or manipulate the hoe nearly as well. I tried to learn . . . but I was unable to master the farming skills. By any standard, I was way below the average of all the boys in terms of farming knowledge and abilities. (pp. 4–5)

What he was good at, Yong discovered, was learning. Or, more specifically, learning languages and technology. Math was not a strong interest or ability for Yong. But, fortuitously, when he was ready to go to college, students could major in foreign languages without passing the math section of the standardized entrance examination. Yong observed:

> I have been fortunate to be able to avoid virtually everything that I have no potential for being good at or I am not interested in. More important, I have been fortunate to have had the space to explore my passions and experiment with different undertakings to discover my weaknesses and strengths. (p. 5)

In *Reach for Greatness*, Yong Zhao challenges the educational status quo as a system that is based upon two basic but flawed assumptions: (1) that "there is a set of skills and knowledge everyone must have in order to live a successful life in the world," and (2) that "all children are capable of and interested in acquiring the skills and knowledge at a similar pace" (p. 8). Instead, he argued that:

1. Changes in society always redefine the value of knowledge and skills and that recent changes brought about by technology have made traditionally valued skills and knowledge obsolete, requiring the need to consider new human qualities;
2. Understandings of human nature and learning suggest that human beings are differently talented, have different desires and interests, and have different experiences that interact with their natural talents and interests to give each person a unique profile of abilities and desires, stronger in some areas and weaker in others; and
3. In a world in which technology has and will continue to replace humans in routine tasks, we need human beings to be unique, creative, and entrepreneurial and an education system that helps every student become uniquely creative and entrepreneurial. (p. 9)

Yong Zhao calls for a new way to think about what we call individualization, arguing that "the education system rarely cares about the children's individual passions or talents" (p. 17) and emphasizes primarily the "talents" of being a good student, following rules, doing homework, getting good grades, and passing tests. A norm-referenced, standardized education process says to children that not *all* of them can be great, since some, by definition, will fall below the average; that not all talents are equally important; and that not all passions are equally valued.

Instead, Zhao suggests, in the 21st century, we can shed the burden of determining who will succeed and who will not, and we can "go for great" for all children. First, we must embrace the idea that every student has their own unique profile of strengths and weaknesses—what Zhao refers to as a jagged profile—and that when everyone is unique, there is no utility whatsoever to the notion of average. Every student can be great in their own way.

Second, we can "go for great" by understanding that all talents are worth developing and all passions worth pursuing (Zhao, 2018). This is a point that Yong fleshed out in one of his earlier books, *World Class Learners: Educating Creative and Entrepreneurial Students* (2012), which I mentioned briefly in Chapter 2, and that bears exploring as we think about this notion of all students having the potential to be great.

When we think about the demands of a future world dominated by (presumably) complex technology and the necessity for seemingly complex higher order cognitive skills (critical thinking), we may envision fewer opportunities for young people with disabilities. But, there is another side to that coin. In *World Class Learners*, Yong notes that because of increased human productivity and the rapid rise of technology, Americans spend much less of their annual income on necessities like food, clothing, and shelter, and substantially more (in fact, more than twice as much as in the 20th century) on everything else. While traditional jobs may be lost in a global, technological economy, jobs will be gained in other largely unidentified domains. Expanding on this in *Reach for Greatness*, Yong noted that, as a result, more and more talents and abilities will have economic importance. He stated:

> Today, in the new age, a majority of traditional routine tasks that required a homogenous set of skills and knowledge are now performed by machines, and human needs have shifted from basic needs to more psychological, aesthetic and intellectual needs. Thus, the full spectrum of human talents has become economically valuable. (Zhao, 2018, p. 57)

Consider what this means for students with disabilities. How many of the jobs that we're worried will go away are low-paying, boring jobs? And, really, how well have we been doing in providing an education that actually enables students with disabilities to obtain even those boring, low-paying jobs? A Harris poll from 2010 found that among working-age people with disabilities, only 21% were employed full- or part-time, and that more than one third of people with disabilities had household incomes of $15,000 or below. I don't know about you, but those numbers suggest to me that we'd better try something else and that what we're doing isn't working very well.

And, let's go beyond the world of work in the 21st century. Every futurist I read makes two common points. First, automation and technology will create less demand for work, as we've known it, and second, as a consequence, our nonwork life will matter more than it does today. Futurists often challenge the notion of work–life balance as being a 20th-century idea. In the 21st century, work and life will merge in ways that are not true today.

Leaders in the fields of career and vocational guidance are having to reshape how they do business. Mark Savickas, whose scholarship has led the way in this field, has pioneered the ideas of career construction and life design as frameworks for 21st-century career and vocational guidance and counseling. The former, career construction, reflects the idea that people will "construct" their own careers. Savickas (2005) identified the central thesis of career construction theory as recognizing that "Careers do not unfold; they are constructed as individuals make choices that express their self-concepts and substantiate their goals in the social reality of a work role" (p. 43).

A life design approach takes the career construction notion one step further. As work and nonwork roles and identities merge, people will need to design their own lives. The notion of work life changes from meaning a distinct life at work to meaning that work and life share equal billing in one's life, not distinct identities. In an article I wrote with colleagues on the application of a life design approach to transition, we noted the need "to design a work life that is satisfying to the individual, and that can be redesigned as needs, interests, life experiences, and opportunities change" and that "accumulated knowledge, skills, and experiences can be invested to create or respond to new opportunities as they arise" (Wehmeyer et al., in press).

So, returning to our conversation about going for great for all children, the first two principles for reaching for greatness are to embrace the idea that all children can be great in their own ways and that all talents are worth developing and passions worth pursuing. The third principle is that all children want to be great. And what educator would dispute that? Of course children want to succeed. Of course they want to have the things they do be recognized and celebrated.

The road to greatness for all children is through what Yong Zhao calls personalizable education, and it is a path I believe we need to travel to move beyond individualization.

PERSONALIZABLE EDUCATION

What is personalizable education and how does it move us beyond individualization? Yong Zhao (2018) argues that "personalizable education is fundamentally different from personalized learning, individualized learning, differentiated instruction, or customized education in a number of ways" (p. 67). Let me begin by describing what personalizable education is, and then return to how it is different from personalized or individualized learning. There are four features of personalizable education: agency, shared ownership, flexibility, and value creation.

Agency

In the realm of education, agency refers to being an actor in one's life, rather than being acted upon. It is closely aligned with the notion of self-determination, about which I will talk more in later chapters. Zhao (2018) stated that "for students to explore, identify and enhance their strengths and follow their passions, they must become owners of their own learning . . . they must have agency in designing their own learning" (p. 58).

When we talk more about self-determination in a later chapter, we'll think about how we promote agency; for now, I think it's important to observe that if we expect young people to navigate a 21st-century "work-life" world, they need to learn the knowledge, skills, and attitudes that will enable them to be agents in their own lives. Further, if we are to restructure education to focus on strengths and passions, that, by its very definition, requires promoting agency.

Years ago I read something that resonated with me. I know it was written by Dorothy Lipsky and Alan Gartner, whose names I mentioned in the Introduction, but for the life of me I cannot find the exact source. Even Google is failing me. The gist was this: If we structured college the way we structure most transition "programs" for students with disabilities, we would have each possible college student take a battery of tests to determine what it was that they did worst and then we would spend 4 years working to get the student a little better at those things they do not do well (and probably don't like).

What personalizable education requires is that we do the opposite; that we approach K–12 education in the same way we approach college. And how is that? When you go to college, you identify a set of things that you think you are interested in and that you might have passion for, and you identify a set of things that you do well. In the Venn diagram of those two sets, there is going to be a subset of things that you do well and that you are interested in or have a passion for. You then spend your time getting a lot better at those things.

Over the 25 years I've talked about the need to promote self-determination for students with disabilities and talked about issues of agency, I periodically have received pushback from professionals who think this means that we should let students do what they want. "They would not even come to school if we let them do what they want," I would hear. Well, first, maybe if we structured schools to provide greater agency, to focus on strengths, and to engage passions and interests, students would choose to come to school. But even beyond that, what we mean by promoting agency can look very different across schools and circumstances.

At a training I was doing once, a clearly agitated professional raised his hand and said very slowly and methodically, "Are you saying that if one of my clients [he was in vocational rehabilitation, not special education] who has diabetes wants to eat a dozen donuts, I should let him, even if it means he'll go into a diabetic coma and possibly die?" After a brief silence—I'll admit I was somewhat stunned—I suggested that he not let that person eat the donuts and die. But, my argument then was and still is now, look at how controlling and dependency-creating far too many schools and other systems with which people with disabilities must interact are, and tell me that there isn't a lot we can do to provide greater choice, volition, and agency.

Personalizable education provides agency at multiple levels and to multiple degrees. The fact is, we don't know how much is too much agency and choice because, frankly, it's not a situation that exists in many schools. I'm interested in going all out with agency, student choice, and opportunities for students to explore strengths and passions and seeing where that leads us.

I had the opportunity to visit a very innovative school in Beijing, China, in 2017 with Yong Zhao. That school, the Beijing Academy, practiced student agency in many ways, but one stuck out to me as particularly reflective of agency. Students had a meaningful role in deciding what content they learned (see Shared Ownership, next), and when it was determined what students would take, they had three options as to how they learned it. Students could learn the content in what was a very traditional manner: in a classroom, with peers, and with a teacher providing instruction. Or students could choose to learn the content in small learning groups with other peers. Or, third, students could choose to engage in a course of self-study that enabled them to learn the content. I saw students in all three learning conditions and was told by school leaders that students often varied how they chose to learn, choosing to learn one content area in a classroom context, another in self-study, and another in a small learning group.

Shared Ownership

The second feature of personalizable education, shared ownership, continues the theme emphasized in agency. And perhaps to assure educators that personalizable learning is not about letting students eat all the donuts they want, as it were, shared ownership emphasizes that students and adults (teachers, administrators, cafeteria workers, para-educators, etc.) are co-owners of what happens in the school.

I mentioned previously how influential Seymour Sarason's writings were in my professional development and growth. In *The Predictable Failure of Educational Reform: Can We Change Course Before It's Too Late*, Sarason (1990) argued that what was predictable about the failure of educational reform as it was rolling out in the 1990s was not related to the need for reform, but the fact that the dominant reforms were vertical in nature. That is, they originated at "higher up" levels (federal government, state government, district leadership, etc.) and at the bottom of that vertical structure were teachers and students.

Think about how the standards-based reform movement unfolded in the late 1990s and early 2000s. Standards were set that reflected what "all" students in our society must know. Curriculum (eventually standardized) was developed to align with those standards, and student performance expectations were set. Assessments were developed to test how well students performed on those standards. And, under the guise of "motivating students," high stakes were determined that essentially punished students who did poorly, the schools they attended, and the teachers who taught them.

Okay, some teachers were involved in determining the standards, setting the curriculum, and creating the assessments, but I don't believe any students were ever consulted with regard to what they should know and how they should learn it, and I know that very few, if any, special educators were involved in standards setting or curriculum development. One can say that this is a system set up to raise expectations for (and performance of) all students, but I believe it is a system that mainly taught some students and their teachers that they would never be great.

Shared ownership not only empowers students, but it empowers educators. And here's one difference between agency and shared ownership. A focus on agency is a focus on the student, enabling students to exert control over their education. When schools emphasize shared ownership, students and teachers care not only about themselves, but about their peers and colleagues.

We're constantly being told that we need to operate schools more like businesses, so what if we operate schools like Hy-Vee supermarkets, the Ferrellgas Partners propane company, or Lifetouch Inc., the company that probably takes the school photos for your yearbook? What might we emulate about those businesses, other than their success? Each is wholly owned by its employees. Shared ownership of schools means that students have agency over learning, but also have shared responsibility for the success of the school. Students have the opportunity to set rules and procedures that impact the school culture and structure, but also are responsible for upholding those rules and facilitating those procedures. Responsibility for strategic planning? Shared. Responsibility for curriculum decisionmaking? Shared. Responsibility for ensuring the quality of the educational experience? Shared.

Beijing Academy, which I mentioned earlier, practiced shared ownership in a myriad of ways. As an example, fieldtrips became a shared responsibility. Students had a voice not only in what fieldtrips were taken, but in planning for the trips, organizing and arranging them, budgeting for expenses, and arranging transportation. Students made proposals to teachers and administrators and, jointly, students, teachers, and school leaders selected those fieldtrips that seemed best to meet the needs of the school or the class.

Flexibility

Personalizable education "must have flexibility as a defining feature" to be able to respond "to new opportunities, emerging needs, and unexpected problems . . . [in] all aspects of the school: leadership, timetable, curriculum, facilities, students, and staffing" (Zhao, 2018, p. 64). Zhao argues that flexibility is first and foremost a mindset, a mindset that "believes in the value of change and that plans, no matter how carefully thought out, will always have unexpected disruptions and/or outcomes that require change" (p. 64).

The fact is, if we are to facilitate agency and shared ownership, we're going to have to be flexible. Yong Zhao (2018) argues that we "are often constrained by what already exists without questioning why it existed," and illustrates this by noting that "many educators feel constrained by timetables and scheduling, but timetables and scheduling were created for education . . . they can be reimagined" (p. 65).

In *Deep Learning: Engage the World Change the World* (2018), Michael Fullan and colleagues argue that we need to cultivate rich learning environments for children that are *driven by* learners' curiosity, teach students to be problem designers, pose problems in which students can be actively involved, and structure schools where learning is about taking risks and a lifelong venture. In these rich learning environments, adults believe children will exceed all expectations and that innovation and creativity are "already in the DNA of every human being" (Fullan et al., 2018, p. 14). Note that these authors say that these rich learning environments are driven by student curiosity, not just "take advantage of" student curiosity.

I want to emphasize another point made by Fullan and colleagues in their discussion of deep learning:

> The "old" notion that students who have struggled with school must wait until they have mastered the foundations of literacy and numeracy are [*sic*] being replaced with effective programs that bolster foundational literacy and numeracy skills but simultaneously engross students in authentic tasks that engage them deeply while providing meaningful ways to learn critical literacy skills. (p. 24)

Flexibility is a mindset that begins with adopting the belief that all children can be great, and then letting student curiosity, passions, and strengths be the driving force for designing classrooms, schedules, routines, curricula, and, in short, schools.

Value Creation

The final defining feature of personalizable education is value creation. Value creation means "guiding students in turning their passions and strengths into something valuable," which in turn makes learning meaningful and gives it purpose. We've recognized the importance of experiential learning since the earliest years of education. But, both personalizable education and deep learning emphasize that we must go beyond traditional forms of experiential learning such as project-based learning or problem-based learning. Value creation involves not just reinforcing learning by engaging in a project or solving a problem, but the active, engaged process of identifying learning needs that align with a student's curiosity: having the student (a) generate ideas and assess existing knowledge and areas of needed learning pertaining to the goal and need, (b) identify resources to address the goal, (c) convince others of the value of the initiative, (d) create a product or service to meet the need or goal, and (e) present and market the product or service.

Value creation implies not just value to the student but value to someone else, infusing meaning and purpose into learning. Fundamentally, value creation cannot exist without student agency and shared ownership; that, perhaps, is how it differs from traditional product- or problem-based learning experiences.

Before we wrap up this chapter, I mentioned earlier that personalizable education differs from the more familiar concepts of personalized learning, differentiated instruction, or customized education. I hope that by now you've sorted out how these ideas differ. Yong Zhao laid out a number of ways that he thinks personalizable education differs from, particularly, personalized learning.

First, Zhao (2018) argues that personalized learning "is about fixing students' deficits . . . [and is] based on the outdated assumption that all students can and should learn the same thing, even if they need to learn at different speeds or perhaps in different ways" (p. 67). This seems somewhat harsh, or at least it did to me when I first read it. But, I will say that my complaint with personalized learning has long been that it seems to be simply a synonym for using technology to learn the same things that students have always had to learn.

The National Center for Learning Disabilities (NCLD) has done a nice job of addressing issues pertaining to the application of personalized learning to students with learning disabilities. In a report titled *Agents of Their Own Success: Self-Advocacy Skills and Self-Determination for Students with Disabilities in the Era of Personalized Learning* (2018), NCLD noted that after a comprehensive review of the literature on personalized learning:

> A theme that consistently emerged was that personalized learning requires students to make good choices about their learning, assert their needs and pursue their goals in order to be successful. These skill sets are vital for all learners, but they are especially important for students with disabilities. Yet these skills are not frequently taught to students, an omission that harms those who need these skills the most. (p. 2)

I had the chance to work with the staff at NCLD and other stakeholders to address the lack of focus on student direction and choice in personalized learning. What Yong Zhao is pointing out is what NCLD found: Personalized learning, as it has rolled out, insufficiently focuses on student choice, voice, creativity, and ownership of learning.

The second difference between personalized learning and personalizable education is that personalizable education emphasizes personalization of outcomes, while personalized learning emphasizes personalization of the process leading to predetermined outcomes. Finally, Zhao (2018) argues that personalized learning restricts student agency to "what is offered by the personalized learning system or instructional practices" (p. 69), which are determined by others, typically teachers or systems. In personalizable education, "personalization is carried out *by* the students, under guidance from adults such as teachers, counselors, and parents" (p. 69, emphasis in original).

Is "going for great" by creating a personalizable education a hokey idea and simply pie-in-the-sky thinking? I don't know. I don't think so. When I opened the latest issue of *Educational Leadership*, published by ASCD (formerly the Association for Supervision and Curriculum Development), on classroom management, I saw these same themes reflected in the articles. The September 2018 issue contained articles titled "Tear Down Your Behavior Chart!" (Jung & Smith, 2018), which spoke to the fact that behavior charts mainly shame children, don't promote self-regulation, and harm some children; "You Don't Know Me Like That" (Benn, 2018), which talked about the need to build rapport and relationships with students; and "Room for Improvement" (Dillon, 2018) about changing how classrooms are designed to build community and caring spaces. And, toward the end of the issue, there was an article titled "Finding Your Classroom's Greatness" (Tinley, 2018). Tracey Tinley is an elementary school teacher in Ontario, Canada. She embraced "going for great" because of a Nike ad campaign titled "Find Your Greatness." Those are the words over the door in Tracey Tinley's classroom. Tinley had observed that her students came to her "with the mindset that learning is a competitive sport" and that even at their young ages, "there are children who have already decided whether they are a 'winner' or a 'loser' at the game of school" (p. 79).

So, Tinley embarked on a school year with every effort to make sure that every student understood the ways in which they were great. Like the best teachers, she just made up much of what she did; she created games and activities that emphasized strength, courage, ability, mastery, and perseverance. Although not in so many words, she created a class that emphasized student agency, shared ownership, flexibility, and value creation. On the final day of that school year, Tinley made a subtle change to the slogan above the classroom door. She changed "Find Your Greatness" to "Found Our Greatness." She wondered if any of her students would notice:

> They noticed. Immediately. As they ran toward me, eager to point out the change, I smiled and assured them that I had known they would find their greatness all along. (Tinley, 2018, p. 81)

I want Tracey Tinley, and all of the other teachers out there like Tracey, to teach all of America's children. I think we can go beyond individualization to create a personalizable education for those children.

CHAPTER 4

Beyond the Continuum

Whole-System Change

I believe that one of the most damaging ideas to be promulgated through P.L. 94-142 was the idea of a continuum of services. Of course, you'll know from my discussion in Chapter 2 that this simply means a continuum of *programs* and that the variable on which the continuum is predicated is degree of segregation. The continuum of services language in IDEA (or, more accurately, the continuum of alternative placements language) and the idea of a least restrictive environment (LRE) are linked in how special education is implemented currently. So, let's begin by seeing exactly what is required when it comes to the continuum and LRE, and then think about how that has played out and what alternatives might move us more in alignment with the objectives for a 21st-century education.

CONTINUUM OF ALTERNATIVE PLACEMENTS

The regulations for IDEA state that

(a) Each public agency must ensure that a continuum of alternative placements is available to meet the needs of children with disabilities for special education and related services.
(b) The continuum required in paragraph (a) of this section must—
(1) Include the alternative placements listed in the definition of special education under §300.39 (instruction in regular classes, special classes, special schools, home instruction, and instruction in hospitals and institutions); and
(2) Make provision for supplementary services (such as resource room or itinerant instruction) to be provided in conjunction with regular class placement. (Sec. 300.115)

So, what does §300.39 say? It says:

(1) Special education means specially designed instruction, at no cost to the parents, to meet the unique needs of a child with a disability, including—
(i) Instruction conducted in the classroom, in the home, in hospitals and

institutions, and in other settings; and

(ii) Instruction in physical education.

Let's take a moment to note that this is how IDEA defines special education: as specially designed instruction. That it has come to mean a place where students go to receive "special education" is a function, I believe, of the deficits/program mentality of the era. Finally, let's look at the least restrictive environment requirements in IDEA:

> (1) Except as provided in §300.324(d)(2) (regarding children with disabilities in adult prisons), the State must have in effect policies and procedures to ensure that public agencies in the State meet the LRE requirements of this section and §§300.115 through 300.120.
>
> (2) Each public agency must ensure that—
>
> (i) To the maximum extent appropriate, children with disabilities, including children in public or private institutions or other care facilities, are educated with children who are nondisabled; and
>
> (ii) Special classes, separate schooling, or other removal of children with disabilities from the regular educational environment occurs only if the nature or severity of the disability is such that education in regular classes with the use of supplementary aids and services cannot be achieved satisfactorily. (Sec. 300.114)

Now, just to be clear, I am not a legal scholar. I have, however, worked with one for years: Rud Turnbull. From Rud (and from Alan Abeson, whom I've mentioned previously) I learned that the language pertaining to LRE is derived from the legal doctrine of *least restrictive alternative*. Here, in my non-attorney explanation, is the gist of this doctrine: If the government is in any way to restrict the liberty and freedom of a citizen, the government has a constitutional obligation to do so "in a way that is least restrictive of the person's liberty itself, in a way that is less drastic than other ways available to the state" (Turnbull as cited in Shogren, Wehmeyer, Martinis, & Blanck, 2019). It was this doctrine upon which the U.S. Supreme Court decision in *Olmstead v. L.C.* (1999) that "unjustified institutional isolation . . . is a form of discrimination" (527 U.S. 581 at 600) was based. The Court was ruling on a case filed by two women with intellectual disability who claimed that the State of Georgia had violated their basic constitutional right to be protected from undue or unnecessary institutionalization.

So, in the LRE requirements, P.L. 94-142 essentially stated the legal principle that students with disabilities had the right to be educated with all other children (i.e., least restrictive alternative) unless the "nature or severity of the disability is such that education in regular classes with the use of supplementary aids and services cannot be achieved satisfactorily."

In that case (that is, if students cannot be successfully educated in regular classes), the continuum of alternative placements requirements in the law allows that students be educated in an alternative setting—special classes, special schools, home instruction, and instruction in hospitals and institutions—that best meets the students' needs.

How many of you thought that what the law requires is that the *nature and severity* of a child's disability are the basis for placement outside the general education setting? It's natural if you did. That is how the system has operated. As I mentioned concerning my own teaching experiences, placement on the "continuum" was (and I would argue still is) based upon the type and severity of a child's disability.

But that's not what the LRE language says, and what is in practice is certainly not in alignment with the least restrictive alternative doctrine; in fact, in my opinion, it is just the opposite. What the LRE language says is that removal from the "regular education environment" is to occur "only if the nature or severity of the disability *is such that education in regular classes with the use of supplementary aids and services cannot be achieved satisfactorily*" (emphasis added).

Letters issued by the Office of Special Education Programs provide guidance to schools to help clarify what isn't defined in the statute or regulations. What is a "regular education environment"? According to OSEP, that refers to regular classrooms, but also other regular school environments, such as the cafeteria, library, gym, or even hallways. And, importantly, it refers to regular education environments in the school the child would attend if the child did not have a disability.

That setting (regular education environments in the school the child would attend if the child did not have a disability) is, according to OSEP, what must be considered first when placement decisions are made. Considered by whom? The child's IEP team.

IDEA doesn't require that IEP teams have information about how a student *already* performed in a regular education environment or about what specially designed instruction or supplementary aids and services were provided in a regular education environment. OSEP has interpreted LRE to mean that the regular education environment, with specially designed instruction and supplementary aids and services, be the first placement option *considered*, but that if the IEP team believes that the student's IEP cannot be implemented satisfactorily (even with supplementary aids and services), then the IEP team can consider alternative placements.

You don't have to guess where I think this all falls apart. It's what I've talked about in the previous three chapters. That is, we have a system that perpetuates deficits-based thinking that results in programs characterized by homogeneous grouping and resulting in standardization and routinization instead of individualization. These decisions are made based not on data and evidence, but on the "beliefs" of IEP team members.

I said in the Introduction that this book is not a criticism of the existing law, and had the process been implemented such that students were served presumptively in general education settings with specially designed instruction and supplementary aids and services, and were "placed" outside those settings only when they were not successful, I'd have less to quibble with. So, it isn't the law I'm criticizing, but the way it has been interpreted and implemented.

INCLUSION: FALSE DICHOTOMIES, SLIPPERY SLOPES, AND OTHER LOGICAL FALLACIES

I haven't said much about inclusion to this point, although it's not hard to read between the lines that I believe in inclusive practices. But, really, I'm no longer very interested in the pro or con inclusion argument. In fact, I think it's an argument that has distracted us for too long and that too often strays into a number of logical fallacies. I'll come back to that in a moment.

First, though, let me state that I believe that IDEA prioritizes educating all students in general education settings. I don't think that's radical thinking. I believe it is what is communicated in the law. Even more strongly, I believe P.L. 94-142 was written with the least restrictive alternative doctrine in mind, so that the government (i.e., schools) cannot deprive children of their "liberty and freedom" (i.e., being with peers in general education settings) unless it is clearly in the child's best interest to do so. So, I believe that inclusion is important.

I know, from the most recent annual report to Congress on the implementation of IDEA (U.S. Department of Education, 2018), that almost 63% of all children ages 6 through 21 spent 80% or more of their day in regular class settings. That's up from about 47% in the 2000–2001 school year, so let's celebrate that. But, it's also sort of like saying that between Babe Ruth and me, we averaged 357 major league home runs across our lives. The statement is true (he had 714, I never had one in little league, much less played in the major leagues!), but it's not helpful.

So, if 63% of children are "included" (i.e., spend 80% of their day in general education settings), is an argument against the continuum outdated? For several reasons, I think it is not. First, let's note that what that figure also means is that 37% of children spend less than 80% of their day in regular education. Next, keep in mind that children with speech and language impairments make up 17.3% of all children ages 6 through 21 receiving special education services. I was unable to find data on how many minutes or hours of services per day, on average, children served under the speech and language impairment category (as the child's primary disability) received. However, a large survey by the American Speech and Hearing Association (ASHA, 2016) indicated that the mean caseload size for a school-based speech and language pathologist (SLP) was 48, and the mean number of hours spent on direct one-on-one (i.e., pullout) speech and language services per week was 19, with an additional average of 5 hours per week on classroom-based services and 3 hours per week on diagnostic services (the rest of the time was spent on paperwork, etc.). That's 27 hours a week on average providing speech and language services of some sort. With the typical direct, pullout speech therapy session lasting 45 minutes, and the fact that SLPs also serve children who have speech and language impairment as a secondary disability category, I have to conclude that most children in this category are getting services a few times a week for less than an hour at a time, at the most. So how relevant is it really to talk about percent of time spent in regular education for these children? The 2018 IDEA report indicates that 86.6% of children served under the speech and language impairment category are served in general education classrooms 80% of the day or more.

And, here's my point. It's not apples and oranges. Since children with speech and language impairments constitute the second highest number of children receiving special education services, how is the fact that they're getting a couple of 45-minute sessions a week, then going back to their regular class, skewing upward the total percentage of children served in the general education setting 80% of the day or more? Heck, I am more interested in why 13% of children with speech and language impairments as a primary diagnosis are spending less than 80% of their day in general education settings.

Or, let's take children with other health impairments (OHI). The IDEA report indicates that 65.6% of children with OHI are served in the general education classroom for 80% of the day or more. That's the third largest group. There are no reliable counts of the types of conditions children served in the OHI category have (or at least I couldn't find any), but we're talking mainly about children with asthma, ADHD, and epilepsy, and then much smaller numbers of children with serious diseases like leukemia, sickle cell anemia, or heart conditions. So, to what degree do children with asthma "need" education outside a general education setting?

Meanwhile, as of 2015, only 16.7% of students served under the category of intellectual disability spend 80% or more of their day in regular education. And even that figure is just an average across states. In Arizona, it's 7.3%. In California, it's 6%. In Illinois, it is only 4.4%. Which states are doing better? In Vermont, it is 42.8%. In Alabama, it is 42.5%. Iowa tops the list at 65.7%.

It is worse for students with multiple disabilities, only 13.4% of whom spend 80% of their day in general education. Almost half (49.7%) of students with intellectual disability are educated in regular classes less than 40% of the day, and only slightly fewer (46.2%) students with multiple disabilities are educated in regular classes less than 40% of the day. Almost a quarter (24.1%) of students with multiple disabilities are educated in other (highly segregated) environments. For students with autism, only 39.8% spend 80% or more of their day in general education, while 33.2% spend less than 40% of their day in general education. Only 53.6% of children with orthopedic impairments spend 80% or more of their day in general education.

Let's talk about students with learning disabilities. The inclusion wars have raged most intensely between advocates for students with extensive support needs (who, as you see above, experience high levels of segregation) and advocates for students with learning disabilities. The latter argue that some students with learning disabilities benefit from resource room or pull-out services to receive practice and get higher dosages of treatments than can be delivered in general education settings. For students with specific learning disabilities, 69.7% are educated in the general education setting for 80% of their day or more, while 22.9% spend 40 to 79% of their day in general education settings. Only 5.5% of students with specific learning disabilities spend less than 40% of their day in general education, with 2% served in "other environments," which include parental placement in private schools.

By and large, one could argue that the intent of IDEA with regard to education of learners with disabilities in regular education environments is, in fact, playing out in the case of students with specific learning disabilities. That hasn't always been the case, of course. In the 1995 OSEP report to Congress for data from the 1992–1993 school year, only 34.8% of students with specific learning disabilities were served in regular class settings 80% or more of the day, while 43.9% were served primarily in resource rooms (i.e., in general education between 40% and 79% of the school day). And, there was considerable variability at that time. Arizona served 75.28% of students with learning disabilities in resource rooms, Colorado served 77.57% of students in that setting, and Iowa served a whopping 95.98% of students with learning disabilities in resource rooms. New Jersey served 42.24% of students with learning disabilities in wholly separate classes (in general education less than 40% of the day), Louisiana did so for 43.76% of students with learning disabilities, and in the District of Columbia 46.70% of students with learning disabilities were in separate classrooms.

Does the above success negate my concerns with the continuum? Should we just wait? Things got better between the 1992 school year and the 2015 school year for students with learning disabilities. But, in the 1992 school year, 7.11% of students receiving services under the (then) "mental retardation" category were educated in the general education setting 80% of their day or more. From 1992 to 2015, that means there was a 9.59% increase. That's a 0.42% increase each year. Let's see, if that continues, it will be during the the year 2129 that the percent of students with intellectual disability in the general education setting for 80% of the day reaches the average of 62.7% for all students with disabilities reported today.

So, it seems fair that even if one group of students has had benefit, the lack of benefit for another group warrants concern. And, are these issues relevant only to students with the most significant cognitive, physical, or sensory impairments? No. Students with emotional disturbance are educated in the general education setting 80% or more of the day at a rate of only 47.1%, and 17% of them are educated in other (highly restrictive) settings. The latter figure is exceeded only by students with multiple disabilities (24%) and students with deaf-blindness (28.6%).

Basically, the more severe the symptoms of the disability (whether they be cognitive, physical, sensory, or behavioral), the more likely one is to be segregated and relegated to the low expectations and homogeneous grouping of the continuum. Is that surprising? Well, not when we organize schools around deficit models and programs. But, is it optimal for all students? The clear answer to that question seems to me to be no.

Why has the pro and con inclusion argument taken so much of our attention and our energy? I know people on both sides of the argument. I like people on both sides of the argument! By and large (there are always exceptions!), advocates of both sides are passionate, smart, dedicated people. But there are a number of logical fallacies that characterize the argument (if not, I should probably add, the arguers). For one, inclusion or not inclusion is a false dichotomy for all but a very small minority of advocates on one side or the other. If a child is seriously ill and needs homebound services, of course being in the general education setting is an illogical option. If a young man has a debilitating anxiety disorder, then a decision not to be in the general education setting may be in his best interest. We've figured out how to structure schools that have reduced the actual need for education out of the general education setting, which we'll discuss next, but can we agree that there is no all-or-nothing solution to this? I know, inclusion advocates talk about "all" children. But here's the thing: When you're advocating for something, you can't blow an uncertain trumpet, as former Notre Dame president Theodore Hesburgh once said. When we're not talking about more than 80% of children in some disability categories being denied the opportunity to be educated with their nondisabled peers, then perhaps we can have a more nuanced call for action.

We also see a fair share of slippery slope elements to both the pro and con sides, and more than a small amount of hasty generalizations. The latter are statements with insufficient evidence to support them. I would suggest that we have no evidence to support the primacy of the segregated model we began with, and we have a growing body of evidence to support that children with disabilities are better off when educated with their peers without disabilities. We have to err, in recognition of the legal requirements for least restrictive alternatives, on the side of less restrictive environments.

Can we do better? How should we arrange schools to support 21st-century learning? Not, I would argue, in segregated settings. And, emerging schoolwide models are providing direction for us. Ironically, it was with students with learning disabilities that the person–environment fit model of disability I talked about earlier really played out in public schools and began to point toward the importance of schoolwide and system wide models. This occurred not so much using the rationale I provided earlier, but based upon a belief that historical ways of determining eligibility as having learning disabilities were flawed (they were based upon deficit approaches, I would note), and that learning disabilities might better be understood as a function of a student's inadequate response to instruction (Vaughn & Fuchs, 2003).

I believe we have the know-how to educate a substantially higher percentage of students—including students with more extensive support needs—in regular education settings. But, we don't. And, I believe that our current structure and system will not serve students with disabilities well in a 21st-century world. So, you ask, how can we go "beyond the continuum" to better prepare learners with disabilities for 2020 and beyond? I think it begins with the schoolwide models that we've adopted as a field, but then goes beyond to incorporate elements of personalizable education. Let's start by looking at schoolwide models in special education.

SCHOOLWIDE MODELS IN SPECIAL EDUCATION

In the mid-1990s, I co-authored a chapter on quality high schools for students with disabilities with my colleague at the University of Kansas, Wayne Sailor. In that chapter Wayne made a point that struck me as true and that has influenced my thinking since. Wayne pointed out that by placing the onus for inclusion on individual teachers and having only the individual classroom as the focus for determining the success or failure of inclusion, we had missed the point that teachers and students and classrooms are part of a larger system within a school, and that the focus for examining the impact of and promoting inclusive practices should be at the school level.

In his 2002 text *Whole-School Success and Inclusive Education*, Wayne and the contributing authors made a compelling case for a whole-school focus. In the years since that text was published, Wayne's work within the Schoolwide Integrated Framework for Transformation process has built on this earlier work. In a 2005 article in *Phi Delta Kappan,* Wayne and his colleague Blair Roger laid out their argument for "rethinking inclusion" with a schoolwide lens, "in which previously specialized adaptations and strategies are used to enhance the learning of all students" (p. 503). Sailor and Roger lay out a number of guiding principles and critical features of schoolwide models:

1. General education guides all student learning.
2. All school resources are configured to benefit all students.

3. Schools address social development and citizenship forthrightly.
4. Schools are democratically organized, data-driven, problem-solving systems.
5. Schools have open boundaries in relation to their families and communities.
6. Schools enjoy district support for understanding an extensive systems-change effort. (pp. 506–508)

Let's talk a little about current schoolwide initiatives that have emerged over the past decade in special education practice and then return to a consideration of how these models prepare us to change our practices to better meet the demands of a 21st-century education.

RESPONSE TO INTERVENTION, POSITIVE BEHAVIOR SUPPORTS, AND MULTI-TIERED SYSTEMS OF SUPPORTS

When I discussed the educational implications for person–environment fit models of disability in Chapter 1, I mentioned that the good news was that we actually have practices that reflect that way of thinking about disability. Perhaps not coincidentally, the major schoolwide models in special education embody the structure of person–environment fit models of disability.

The Response to Intervention (RTI) initiative was designed to provide an alternative way to identify students with specific learning disabilities. The major benefit to the RTI process, argued advocates, was that it did not wait for the child to fail before providing necessary supports. Within RTI, the focus is on the use of frequent, repeated measures of individual students' or groups of students' academic progress (using a progress-monitoring system) and using those data to make decisions about the need for more intensive supports and interventions. RTI models use a "tiered" intervention process, where Tier 1 refers to high-quality instruction provided to all students, Tier 2 refers to more intensive interventions provided to a smaller subset of students (often in small groups) who are not benefiting from Tier 1 instruction, and Tier 3 interventions refer to the most intensive, often one-on-one interventions for students who do not respond to Tier 2 interventions.

Although initially intended to replace the process for identifying students with specific learning disabilities, RTI became more widely adopted as a means for educating learners who are struggling, without the need for diagnosis and classification. The National Association of State Directors of Special Education issued a report in 2005 that identified the core assumptions of RTI as including that the educational system can teach all children effectively, that a problem-solving model should be used to make decisions about tiered interventions, and that assessment must be used to inform instruction.

Can you see the direct relationship between RTI and person–environment fit models of disability? The "environment" in RTI is the instruction used to ensure that all children learn academic content. In traditional special education models, what changes if the child doesn't learn is too often the child's placement (at least for children who have had the chance to be in the general education setting). In RTI, what changes is the type, intensity, duration, and dosage of the intervention. Presumably, within RTI the general education environment (broadly cast as all of the school) is the setting in which all children are educated. Even children who need Tier 3 interventions to succeed are educated in the general education setting for the majority of their day.

Although the development of RTI occurred during the last quarter of the 20th century, it was its inclusion in the 2004 reauthorization of IDEA that really propelled its wide adoption. Emerging at roughly that same time was a second schoolwide model, positive behavior supports, focused not on academic performance but on reducing disruptive and problem behavior. I am sure most special educators are familiar with PBS so I'm not going to describe it in any detail, other than to note some of its features that tie into person–environment fit models of disability.

First, let's dispose of the misconception that PBS is an intervention or practice. It's not; it is a schoolwide model that combines multiple practices. George Sugai, one of the pioneers in PBS, and his colleague Brandi Simonsen stated that PBS is a "framework or approach that provides the means of selecting, organizing and implementing . . . evidence-based practices" (2012, p. 4).

My favorite definition of PBS is the one I mentioned in a prior chapter, from Ted Carr and Rob Horner and a whole slew of folks who were involved in the early development of PBS. In a review of the literature published in 1999, Carr and colleagues defined PBS "as an approach for dealing with problem behavior that focuses on the remediation of deficient contexts (such as environmental conditions and/or behavioral repertoires) that by functional assessment are documented to be the source of the problem" (p. 1).

Many people think that PBS is about the remediation of problem behaviors. It's not. It's about changing the context so that problem behaviors are no longer necessary or effective. It's about addressing the environmental context to determine what is causing the person to engage in behavior that is perceived as problem behavior, and what the person is communicating by engaging in that behavior; fixing or modifying the context as needed; and providing alternatives that will enable the person to get what they need and want in ways that are more acceptable to society.

PBS was the first large initiative to use the term *supports*. The practices and procedures (supports) that make up PBS range from systematic analysis of the function of the behavior and what is motivating it, the use of behaviorally oriented strategies that focus on positive reinforcement of positive or adaptive behavior, and schoolwide implementation that includes making sure every student knows the rules, supporting students to understand the rules, and creating a positive atmosphere. Like RTI, PBS adopted a tiered approach, usually referred to as primary, secondary, and tertiary. Tier 1 interventions are intended to support all students to be successful, behaviorally, in schools. Tier 2 interventions are intended to support students who need more intensive supports than most students receive. And, Tier 3 interventions are typically intensive supports for students who need that.

It was probably inevitable that these tiered models would merge, and that is essentially what is referred to as multi-tiered systems of supports, or MTSS. Schools care about both academic performance and behavior. MTSS systems use the tiered approaches and interventions in RTI and PBS to create a schoolwide approach to supporting more positive academic and behavioral outcomes for all learners who are struggling.

WHOLE-SYSTEM CHANGE

One can see many of the elements of personalizable education inherent in RTI, PBS, and MTSS—flexibility, emphasis on student strengths, and value creation. So, it is relevant to ask whether our existing schoolwide models are sufficient for 21st-century education. Not yet, I think, for two reasons.

First, there have been a string of initiatives—from mainstreaming to the regular education initiative to inclusion, to, even, the access to the general education curriculum initiative—that ultimately have fallen short of the objective of merging special and general education. Why have these had incremental success, at best? Well, there are probably a lot of reasons, but one that stands out is that these have been special education initiatives with little or no buy-in, apparently, from general education.

Second, although these schoolwide special education models embody elements of personalizable education, they do not share the same focus. PBS, RTI, MTSS—they are system changes that are focused on enabling students to achieve predetermined outcomes. Much as was argued by Yong Zhao about the ways in which personalizable education differs from personalized learning, none of the existing schoolwide models truly embrace the features of shared ownership and agency. That's not to say, perhaps, that they could not; it is just to say that as they currently are implemented, they go only so far in that.

Further, I think it is important to return to the points made by Voulgarides (2018) in her analysis of the role of compliance in addressing racial disproportionality in special education. That is, we can implement these schoolwide efforts, but if they are tied to understandings of disability that are deficits-based and do not take into account the multiple, varied factors that influence learning, we run the risk of simply falling into a program/

compliance mentality yet again. Researchers exploring the interactions of teachers with students in classrooms in elementary schools in which PBS was implemented found that despite the overall schoolwide emphasis of positive reinforcement within PBS, teachers had a higher overall mean for reprimands than either general (class-wide) or student-focused praise (Reinke, Herman, & Stormont, 2013). PBS or MTSS or any other school-wide approach that does not also incorporate the big ideas we've discussed previously will, likely, be insufficient.

But, the good news is that system-wide change is at the heart of 21st-century learning initiatives like Michael Fullan's deep learning and Yong Zhao's personalizable education. We have an opportunity, I think, to join forces with general education in whole-system change to benefit all children. These 21st-century education initiatives are general education initiatives, but we have knowledge and skills that will be needed if these initiatives are to be successful.

Fullan and colleagues (2018) emphasize that the whole-system change needed in education to accomplish deep learning is "a transformation of the culture of learning. . . . The mindset we are fostering together is whole system change and deep learning for everyone" (p. 117). Recall, if you will, that deep learning is defined as learning that "situates the learner as some-one who acts upon the world (usually with others) thereby transforming her or himself *and* the world itself" (p. xvii, emphasis in original), that "increases student engagement in the learning through personalization and ownership," and that "connects students to the 'real world,' which is often more reflective of their own reality and cultural identity" (p. 9).

Think back to Yong Zhao's discussion of shared ownership and flexi-bility as critical elements of personalizable education. These are "whole-sys-tem" elements of change. By whole system, Zhao refers not only to educators, whether at the district, school, or classroom levels, but to every layer that impacts education. Governments need to "retreat from overgoverning," and particularly "get away from determining what, when, and where all stu-dents should be taught" (Zhao, 2018, p. 76). Schools need to embrace and teachers need to emphasize qualities that support personalizable education, such as:

1. Ability to identify strengths and passions.
2. Ability to inspire and challenge.
3. Empathy and emotional intelligence.
4. A broad and long-term perspective of education.
5. Resourcefulness and collaboration.

So let's say that we go "beyond the continuum" by collaborating with all educators who are engaged in changing mindsets and in whole-system change that emphasizes the principles of personalizable education, and particularly, perhaps, in building schoolwide systems that focus on strengths, are driven by students' curiosity and passions, emphasize agency and shared ownership, create value, and encourage flexible mindsets. And, rather than trying to force yet another special education reform onto an unwilling general education, we can bring our capacity to educate all learners, including struggling learners, to the table.

CHAPTER 5

Beyond Textbooks

Technology and Universal Design for Learning

In its 1982 decision in *Board of Education of the Hendrick Hudson Central School District, Westchester County v. Rowley*, the U.S. Supreme Court held that what was then still called the Education for All Handicapped Children Act guaranteed a "substantively adequate program of education to all eligible children," and that this requirement would be satisfied if the child's IEP set out an educational program that was "reasonably calculated to enable the child to receive educational benefits."

Let's be self-reflective here. Did we get into the field of special education to provide a "substantively adequate" education for children with disabilities? Is our professional ambition to ensure that students with disabilities have an educational program from which they might "reasonably" benefit? What the ruling said, or at least how it played out over the next quarter-century, was that there was no guarantee of a quality education, just the guarantee of a potential for benefit. And, really, over time, any accountability that we've been held to has been a process accountability; did we get the paperwork in on time, did we invite the right people to the IEP, did we dot every "i" and cross every "t" in the IEP?

That has never sat very well with me. And, far too often, I think that we worry more about the paperwork than about the quality of the education. As I discussed earlier, individualization doesn't guarantee quality, nor does, in this case, adherence to process standards.

As what became IDEA was reauthorized, however, requirements that seemed to expect more than just "possible benefit" and a "substantially adequate" education were written into the law. In the 1997 reauthorization, what came to be known as the access to the general education curriculum mandates appeared, and those were strengthened in the 2004 reauthorization. Section 300.347(a)(3) of the 1997 IDEA required that the IEP of every student receiving special education services include:

A statement of the special education and related services and supplementary aids and services to be provided to the child, or on behalf of the child, and a statement of the program modifications or supports for school personnel that will be provided for the child
(i) to advance appropriately toward attaining the annual goals;

(ii) to be involved and progress in the general curriculum; and

(iii) to be educated and participate with disabled and non-disabled children.

I think it's important to reflect on (i), (ii), and (iii). I would wager that a large number of special educators think the IEP pertains mainly to (i): identifying special education services related to goals that are set. The IEP, as I've mentioned before, too often has constituted an alternative curriculum for students with disabilities.

But, as reflected in the language in part (ii) above, what IDEA requires is that all students receiving special education services be *involved with and show progress in the general curriculum*. The term *access to the general curriculum* refers to this requirement for student involvement and progress, but is not actually the language in the law. Shortly after these mandates were released, I was invited to participate in an advisory group convened by the Office of Special Education Programs, which of course is responsible for the full implementation of IDEA. The purpose of this group was to provide recommendations to OSEP about how to make sure the requirements were met. Also on that panel was Thomas Gilhool, who at that time was staff attorney at the Public Interest Law Center of Philadelphia. Gilhool was a former Secretary of Education for the Commonwealth of Pennsylvania and, what those of us in the field of special education should know (but increasingly do not), was the lead attorney in *PARC v. Commonwealth of Pennsylvania* in 1972, the landmark case that literally set the precedent for the doctrine of a free and appropriate public education as a right for students with disabilities and that provided much of the structure for P.L. 94-142.

Most of us on the panel thought that the new requirements were a positive step, despite our concerns about the emerging standards-based, high-stakes testing policy with which these requirements were aligned. We thought they were a good idea because they could raise expectations for the education of students with disabilities. I've argued in other venues that these mandates introduced a "third generation" of inclusive practices. First-generation inclusive practices focused on getting students into the general education classroom/setting (with mixed success, as was discussed in the previous chapter). Second-generation inclusive practices focused on the development of instructional strategies to teach students with disabilities in general education classrooms (e.g., differentiated instruction, co-teaching, cooperative learning, etc.). Both of these are important, but they focus mainly on where a student is taught. The access to the general education curriculum mandates focused on *what* students were taught. Now, just to be clear, our own research and that of others has shown conclusively that the place where students with disabilities are involved with the general education curriculum is the general education classroom. Students educated in segregated classrooms are much more likely to receive an alternative curriculum (defined by the IEP) that is not linked to the general education curriculum.

But, back to Tom Gilhool. As I said, most of us on the panel believed that the mandates were a good thing and would raise expectations for students with disabilities. I personally saw these as a way to break the logjam with regard to including students with more extensive support needs in general education settings. But Tom Gilhool was not happy. Oh, I think he was fine with the language in the law. What he was livid about was that OSEP officials had begun referring to these mandates as the "access to the general education curriculum" mandates. His argument, and I agree with him, was that access was weak language. The law requires that students with disabilities be *involved with* and *progress in* the general education curriculum. Those are active, aggressive steps. The mandates should have made school districts and special educators stand up and take notice. That students with disabilities needed to make progress in the general education curriculum invoked high stakes indeed.

But, of course, that's not what happened. Now, let me say first that there were very positive outcomes from the involvement and progress requirements. OSEP funded a number of projects that began to rethink how to teach math, reading, and science to students with disabilities, including students with intellectual disability or more extensive support needs. There has been more focus on teaching core content to students with extensive support needs over the past 10 years than during the first 35 years of IDEA's implementation. And, intervention development and evaluation research from this line of work shows clearly that students can acquire knowledge and skills pertaining to these areas. Part of that equation has been the application of Universal Design for Learning and technology in these efforts, and we'll talk more about that shortly, but a big part of it was just that people tried things they had not tried before.

When I was being trained as a special educator, there was a widely held belief that students with intellectual disability hit a "plateau" in what they could learn. That is, there was some level to which they could learn, and it was futile to try to teach them something beyond that. So, we quit trying to teach students to read and focused on so-called functional skills. Of course, reading is the most "functional" skill one could acquire. We defaulted, essentially, to teaching "functional reading" (flash cards with safety words, etc.) for students labeled with intellectual disability. A classic example of the impacts of deficit thinking, in my opinion. Because, of course, the idea of a plateau is pure and utter hogwash. Sure, all of us slow down in what we learn as we get older, but when we're interested in something, we learn it. Students with disabilities can keep learning and making progress in areas like math, reading, and science. What needs to change is how we try to teach those skills. Again, we'll return to that issue, which is at the heart of this chapter's topic, in a moment. I want to finish up this section talking about how a recent Supreme Court ruling should move us away from the *Rowley*-era tyranny of low expectations, striving only for adequacy, and ensuring only the potential for benefit.

In its 2018 ruling in *Endrew F. v. Douglas County School District*, the U.S. Supreme Court stated that "to meet its substantive obligation under the IDEA, a school must offer an IEP reasonably calculated to enable a child to make progress appropriate in light of the child's circumstances"; that a "child's educational program must be appropriately ambitious in light of his circumstances"; that "every child should have the chance to meet challenging objectives"; and that the IEP "is not a form document" and is "constructed only after careful consideration of the child's present levels of achievement, disability, and potential for growth."

The court said this:

> When all is said and done, a student offered an educational program providing "merely more than de minimis" progress from year to year can hardly be said to have been offered an education at all. For children with disabilities, receiving instruction that aims so low would be tantamount to "sitting idly . . . awaiting the time when they were old enough to 'drop out.'"

BEYOND DE MINIMIS

Why did I start this chapter with a recitation on *Rowley* and *Endrew*, adequacy versus challenging objectives, and access versus progress? I did so because it was the 1997 involvement and progress mandates that really launched the focus on UDL in the education of students with disabilities.

From 2002 to 2004, I served on the National File Format Technical Panel established by OSEP through a contract awarded to CAST (formerly the Center for Applied Special Technology). This 40-member panel included representatives from a number of disability groups, technology specialists, and publishers. The intent was to solve a basic problem: Children with print disabilities (blindness, some physical disabilities or learning disabilities) who were eligible to receive alternative format materials (Braille, large print, etc.) were not receiving such materials in a timely manner. We heard stories of students with visual impairments having to wait 6 months before the textbook for their class was available to them in Braille format. It's hard to show progress when you can't be involved with the content.

The panel recommended a set of formatting requirements that publishers needed to meet when publishing anything that would be used for instructional purposes. These requirements, included in the 2004 IDEA reauthorization as the National Instructional Materials Accessibility Standard (NIMAS), ensured that instructional materials would be available in digital formats that could be easily converted to presentation modes that were accessible for students with print disabilities. Also through IDEA 2004, OSEP established the National Instructional Materials Access Center to which publishers submit NIMAS-compliant digital versions of instructional materials and from which states, districts, and, eventually, students can obtain appropriate versions of instructional materials.

Participating in the NIMAS process made me aware that for many students, problems with how content is delivered—written texts, lectures with written notes/presentations, and so on—constitutes the primary barrier to their benefiting from instruction. By 2002, CAST had already pioneered (with funding from OSEP) the idea of Universal Design for Learning. That tackled the issue of the lack of fit between instructional materials (and presentation of and student response to content) and student capacity to be involved with those materials. Remember our discussion from Chapter 1 about person–environment fit models? This was a perfect example. The "environment," in this case, involved instructional materials. The question was how we could reduce the gap between what students could do and what the task required. The answer was: Change the nature, form, and delivery of the instructional content.

Adopting principles of UDL and exploiting the potential of technology are part of how we can go "beyond de minimis" in educating students with disabilities. Personalizable education emphasizes agency, shared ownership, flexibility, and value creation, and UDL and technology are part of promoting agency and ensuring flexibility.

I want to note, before going further, that I think one unfortunate outcome of the UDL movement is that it has been associated almost exclusively with technology use. It is true that technology provides powerful ways to ensure that students can be involved with materials providing content information. But so can common, everyday, nontechnology-based pedagogical practices. Advance organizers, which present big ideas or summaries of content to be covered during a unit or in a book chapter, provide a way of organizing content to support students who otherwise might have a difficult time identifying the important content in a long chapter or unit. It is a form of UDL that has nothing to do with technology.

UNIVERSAL DESIGN FOR LEARNING

I suspect that most readers of this book already know quite a bit about UDL, so it is not my intent to go into any great depth on its principles. Instead, I want us to think about what adopting a UDL mindset gets us with regard to implementing a personalizable education. As I mentioned before, researchers at CAST pioneered the notion of UDL. Its genesis was based upon earlier efforts related to principles of universal design as applied first to architecture, and then to the development of consumer products and, eventually, assistive and other forms of technology.

The principle of universal design in architecture suggested, quite simply, that all buildings/environments should be accessible to all people without the need for modification or adaptation. Buildings are designed with adequate ramps, wide doors, or accessible restrooms, and products are designed with simple controls and clearly understandable uses. A group of architects, product developers, engineers, and other stakeholders forwarded seven principles of universal design through the Center for Universal Design at North Carolina State University in 1997. These were:

Principle 1: Equitable use
Principle 2: Flexibility in use
Principle 3: Simple and intuitive use
Principle 4: Perceptible information
Principle 5: Tolerance for error
Principle 6: Low physical effort
Principle 7: Size and space for approach and use

You can find a lot more information about these principles online, if you're not already familiar with them. But, they are fairly self-evident. Equitable use refers to designs that can be used by a wide array of people with diverse capacities; flexibility refers to the design's adaptability across different people and uses; tolerance for error refers to designs that allow users to make a mistake and still be able to use the device, and so forth. See the pattern? Universal design is about designs. It is about designing environments or products so that people across the spectrum of abilities and capacities can use them without modification.

The key is the word *design*. It's not about adapting something to make it usable by someone. Having to build a ramp so someone who uses a wheelchair can access a building is not universal design. Building a building that has ramps already installed, is. How many times have you wanted to use a new microwave and found that you couldn't figure out how to do something as simple as heat up your coffee? Not very well designed for simple and intuitive use. How about setting an alarm clock? For years, until my smartphone became my alarm clock, I would carry a windup alarm clock with me in my suitcase because five times out of ten I could not figure out how to set the alarm using the ultra-fancy alarm clock in the hotel room.

So, as the field of special education began to think about promoting student involvement in content instruction, and as person–environment fit models of understanding disability began to proliferate, it is not surprising that the idea of universal design was brought to the development of instructional materials.

CAST proposed three principles pertaining to the design of learning environments (the curriculum, how students respond to it, and the environment). You can learn more about this framework at www.cast.org, and I'm not going to go into any detail. The three principles are that the learning environment should provide multiple means of student engagement, multiple means of representation, and multiple means of action and expression (Rose & Meyer, 2002). These principles of UDL align well with the elements of personalizable education. Providing multiple means of engagement includes tapping into a student's interests and preferences, optimizing student agency, and promoting student self-regulation and self-directed learning. Perhaps the most recognized principle of UDL, providing multiple means of representation, really refers to flexibility in how instructional materials and environments are designed to provide multiple means of content delivery, support understandings of how content materials interact with and relate to one another and what the big ideas are, and present content in multiple ways (e.g., video, audio, digital, print, etc.). Providing multiple means of action and expression refers to accommodating the various ways students respond to content and express what they know, and promoting agency through goal setting and attainment.

David Rose, Anne Meyer, and their colleagues at CAST have been pioneers in UDL. I'll confess, though, that my favorite definition of UDL was from Kathleen McLane and Ray Orkwis, both of whom were working in the publication department at the Council for Exceptional Children. They defined UDL as:

> the design of instructional materials and activities that allows learning goals to be achievable by individuals with wide differences in their abilities to see, hear, speak, move, read, write, understand English, attend, organize, engage, and remember. (Orkwis & McLane, 1998, p. 9)

I like this definition because, first, it's clear that UDL is about the design of instructional materials and activities. Second, it states up front that it is about designs that enable learners across a wide array of abilities to learn. Finally, if one thinks about supporting students with differences in *their abilities to see, hear, speak, move, read, write, understand English, attend, organize, engage, and remember*, that makes it about every student in schools, not just students with disabilities.

The more I learned, through my time on the NIMAS panel and then in my interactions with researchers at CAST, about UDL and what was possible with regard to the use of technology to present content area, the more I came to recognize that what needed to change, if we were to achieve the intent of the IDEA involvement and progress language, was the way we thought about instruction, from the materials that we used to our expectations for students. The person–environment fit models provided a way to think about disability within a context that emphasized strengths and raised expectations, and practices like UDL (as well as PBS and MTSS, as discussed previously) provided models for how to achieve better outcomes. These are paths that take us beyond de minimis, to use the Supreme Court's language.

Like many other Americans, it took me a long time to actually finish the great American novel, *Moby Dick*. In fact, I will confess that I listened to it on a series of CDs during a particularly long automobile trip. Multiple means of representation, remember? UDL helps everyone! It happens that my favorite title from among the journal articles I've published also invokes Ahab and the great white whale. My colleagues at AbleLink Technologies in Colorado Springs were evaluating the use of a cognitively accessible portable reading system (called Rocket Reader) by adolescents and young adults with intellectual disability. We asked participants in the study what they thought about the Rocket Reader system. Respondents indicated that they had liked using the system, that it was easy, and that they liked using the computer to read. One participant, though, went right to the heart of the matter. When asked whether he liked the Rocket Reader system, he answered immediately, "*Moby Dick* is my favorite!" That became part of the title of our article. It was ideas underlying the principles of UDL that provided that man access to a great American story, and it was technology that was the platform for his access to the age-old tale of obsession, good and evil, nature and God, life and death, and adventure.

TO INFINITY AND BEYOND

Technology will impact dramatically how we educate students with disabilities. It has already begun to do so, although only in limited ways in most schools. Let me establish up front that I am not an educational technology guru. I know next to nothing about virtual reality or massive open online courses or machine learning. What I do know is that everything I read about technology indicates that it is all about promoting student autonomy and self-direction, peer-to-peer learning, collaboration, and access to data to make decisions.

Let's not even talk about smartphones and tablets. They're becoming ubiquitous in education, and you likely have a sense of some of the things that they can do to support personalizable education's emphasis on flexibility, agency, shared ownership of learning, and value creation. Most futurists agree that the devices we use will become less important anyway. The growth of cloud-based technologies will soon make the specific device you use irrelevant, as all personalization features will reside in the cloud and you will be able to access them anywhere, with any type of device. Think about how Amazon's Alexa, Apple's Siri, and Google's Home Assistant are changing how we use computers. Amazon is banking big on Alexa, making microwave ovens controllable by voice instructions through its Echo gadgets.

But there is more: 3D printing will, in the next several years, change the face of manufacturing. In the United States, NASA is experimenting with 3D printing to "print" complex rocket parts. Futurists predict that in 50 to 75 years, we will have bio-printed organs. When I was a classroom teacher, one of my student's mother was a physical therapist, so she was always at the cutting edge of getting him adapted clothing to enable him to get dressed more independently, like Velcro tennis shoes. She had to buy them from a medical equipment catalog, and even with her professional discounts, they were very expensive. And then, sneaker companies decided that everyone would benefit from Velcro tennis shoes, and when they came to a mass market, the prices for a pair of tennis shoes plummeted. Not only did my student benefit, but so did a lot of elderly people.

So, instead of paying high prices for specialized products (Velcro tennis shoes, speech/communication devices) or having to buy mass-produced products that do not fit the needs of every person, 3D printing will allow people with disabilities to manufacture exactly what they need to be supported to live, learn, work, and play in their communities. A company in London recently marketed 3D printed wheelchairs that can be custom fit and ready in 2 weeks at substantially lower costs than traditionally manufactured commercial wheelchairs.

Finally, you may have heard of the *Internet of Things* or the *Internet of Everything*. This is the idea that someday, and that day will be sooner rather than later, everyday objects, people, processes, and data will be networked and connected such that what you cannot do will be irrelevant; what will matter, will be the supports available for you to succeed. In 2015, it was estimated that about 10 billion objects were connected to the Internet; by 2020, that figure is estimated to be 50 billion objects. If you can't drive, it won't matter, because cars will drive themselves; Google glass and Apple watch are only the tip of the iceberg for wearable computing; in the future, you will no longer need to open your garage door because the traffic signal near your home will sense your car and you in your car, and signal to the garage door that you are approaching. Your garage door opener will recognize you and your car; you will have a trusted, secure identity that can be validated instantly by multiple systems that will negate the need to identify yourself, for example, to health care professionals to access medical records. If you have set it to do so, the garage door opener will communicate with your oven to begin preheating for dinner and with your thermostat to turn down the temperature to cool the house off now that you're home. And so on and so on and so on.

And as these technologies become infused into schools and classrooms, student agency and ownership will be greatly facilitated. And how we teach will have to change. That this is the case is illustrated by innovations in adult and in online and distance learning. We talk about pedagogy in education. The word is from the Greek words for child and leader or tutor. So, pedagogy means leading children, and it is really a description of teacher-directed learning. Adults (teachers) lead or teach children. Even 50 years ago, however, the field of adult education figured out that adult learning is different. Thus, the field of andragogy (leading or teaching man) emerged with an emphasis on student-directed learning. The focus in andragogy is that adults are driven by their curiosity to take initiative in learning and can be taught to use processes that enable them to self-direct learning.

But, even self-directed learning is not enough as online and distance learning becomes more frequent and new technologies are introduced. Thus, the field of open education, focused on online and distance learning, has adopted a focus on heutagogy. That means discovered learning or self-determined learning. Blaschke (2012) observed:

> Pedagogical, even andragogical, educational methods are no longer fully sufficient in preparing learners for thriving in the workplace, and a more self-directed and self-determined approach is needed, one in which the learner reflects upon what is learned and how it is learned and in which educators teach learners how to teach themselves. (p. 57)

Sound familiar? It's a focus on personalizable education. We'll return to the topic of self-determination and self-determined learning in subsequent chapters. For now, just note that as technology is rapidly adopted by and influences education, it will necessitate a focus on student agency, ownership, and flexibility.

THE DIGITAL DIVIDE

We've done some research on the use of technology by students and adults with cognitive disabilities. The first time we examined this was in the late 1990s, and we found that people with cognitive disabilities greatly underutilized technology, even though they and their families recognized that they would benefit from it. We repeated this study in 2012, and while technology usage was higher, it was still well below what one sees in the general public.

I think if we were to repeat this study today or in 2020, we'd continue to see improvement. First, one of the barriers to technology adoption has always been cost. And, one of the characteristics of the market is that costs for devices will be driven down as more people use the devices. Most tablet PCs are now affordable for a larger segment of society than were, for example, desktop PCs when we did the survey in the 1990s.

Another barrier to technology adoption by people with disabilities is device complexity. Think about UDL and its principles. Now think about microwaves and hotel alarm clocks! We reviewed almost 500 studies of the use of technology by people with cognitive disabilities to determine the degree to which the seven principles of universal design, listed previously, were present in the technology being used. The overwhelming majority of devices evaluated had none of these features.

What are some of the features of technology design that are critical to ensure use by people with disabilities? Perhaps the most obvious is simplicity of use. Unfortunately, simplicity and technology seem too often to be incompatible. Such complexity may render an otherwise useful device unusable for a student with a disability, unless the design takes this into account from the start. Of course, flexibility, intuitiveness of use, and all the other principles are important as well.

Educational technology needs to be accessible to all students. I had a good friend, Ray, who was a man with cerebral palsy. Ray was able to talk, but he wasn't easy to understand, and as he got older, it became increasingly difficult to understand what he was saying. A speech therapist finally convinced Ray that he could benefit from an augmentative communication device. At the time, the state-of-the-art devices were relatively large (12" x 18") and were heavier than today's versions. The device that Ray's vocational rehabilitation office bought for him was very high-tech, extremely sophisticated, and completely unusable by him. For one, had he used a wheelchair or a scooter, it could have been mounted on that and been fine. But, Ray walked with a rather awkward gait, and he had to wear the device on a strap around his neck and shoulders, and when he walked, it would whack up against him. That wasn't good for the device or for Ray. Further, it was quite complex to program, and Ray struggled to input messages, relying on friends to program in what he wanted to say. Not very universally designed, certainly. It's not surprising that Ray abandoned the device and relied on friends to interpret for him when needed.

What I learned from the NIMAS panel and my work and interaction over the years with UDL and technology was that we needed to go "beyond textbooks." If you don't read well or don't read at all, you simply cannot be involved with important content information, much less make progress. We used to blame the child for that. With person–environment fit models, we can look at the environment and find ways to use supports to close the gap between what a student can do and what the task demands. This is more than just replacing print texts with digital texts, although that is certainly a start. Closing the gap involves harnessing the full capacity of technology to complement instruction and to drive agency, ownership, and flexibility in personalizable education, and promote self-determined learning. We'll come back to themes of promoting self-determination and autonomy in subsequent chapters. For now, though, I want to stay with the theme of what technology might enable us to do, and talk about the important role of assessment in educating learners with disabilities.

CHAPTER 6

Beyond Testing

Assessment for Growth and Mastery

Assessment and instruction are intimately linked. You can't know what to teach until you know what a student knows. P.L. 94-142 addressed this in part by requiring that the IEP of each child include "a statement of the present levels of educational performance of such child." This went by the awkward acronym of PLEP. It was replaced in the 2004 reauthorization of IDEA with the "present level of academic achievement and functional performance" requirement, which goes by the even-more ungainly acronym of PLAAFP. The PLAAFP section of the IEP serves two purposes. First, a child with a disability is defined in IDEA as a child diagnosed with a specific disability (intellectual disability, learning disability, autism, etc.) who is in need of specially designed instruction because of that disability. The PLAAFP section is intended to show how the child's disability impacts learning (and thus justifies special education services). Second, the PLAAFP section provides assessment data and information for identifying specially designed instruction, supplementary aids and services, and needed goals.

For our purposes, I want to focus on the use of PLAAFP to provide information to be used for instruction rather than diagnosis. We'll return to this in a moment, but let me also mention the other use of testing that dominated education throughout the 2000s and is still part of the national educational landscape: the use of standardized state tests to improve student performance.

There really has never been much controversy over whether making high-stakes decisions about students with disabilities using a one-shot, standardized test is a good idea. Any support for involvement of students with disabilities in statewide testing was related to the potential positive effects of holding students to high expectations, and to a fear that if excluded from such testing, students with disabilities would be further marginalized. In an influential report titled *High Stakes: Testing for Tracking, Promotion, and Graduation* (1999), the National Research Council suggested that for any student, high-stakes decisions should never be based only on a single test, and that this was even more problematic for students with disabilities. The report stated:

Because a test score may not be a valid representation of the skills and achievements of students with disabilities, high stakes decisions about these students should consider other sources of evidence, such as grades, teacher recommendations, and other examples of student work. (p. 295)

With the reauthorization of the Elementary and Secondary Education Act in December 2015 (retitled the Every Student Succeeds Act [ESSA]), the pendulum with regard to high-stakes testing began to swing back. But the law still requires that all students participate in state assessments linked to challenging academic content standards in math, reading or language arts, and, increasingly, science. IDEA gives IEP teams the power to determine whether a student with a disability can take the state assessment without the need for accommodations and, if not, what accommodations might be necessary. Students with the most significant cognitive disabilities, defined in ESSA as the 1% of students in schools who cannot take the state assessment even with accommodations, are allowed to participate in an alternative assessment based upon alternative academic achievement standards. These alternative academic achievement standards must be aligned with content standards established for all students and promote student involvement in the general education curriculum.

I bring all this up mainly because later in this chapter I want to talk about a new way of thinking about assessment that has emerged from a federally funded project called Dynamic Learning Maps, which initially was intended to provide better alternative assessments for the 1% of students who could not take the regular assessment even with accommodations, but has much broader implications for assessment. So, for the moment, let's just note that high-stakes testing is a bad idea for students with disabilities (and probably for all students) and that building a strengths-based, personalizable education is actually counter to the idea of a standardized, high-stakes testing educational system.

POTENTIAL FOR GROWTH

In the U.S. Supreme Court *Endrew F.* decision, which we talked about in the previous chapter, the court essentially added a third intent to the PLAAFP process. The court said that "an IEP is not a form document. It is constructed only after careful consideration of the child's present levels of achievement, disability, and potential for growth." Look at that statement now in light of the requirements for the PLAAFP that we've discussed. The current purposes of the PLAAFP are to confirm the need for specially designed instruction (i.e., confirm the child's eligibility as having a disability under IDEA) and to provide information for goals to be set in the IEP. The third element in the *Endrew* ruling is that information must be used to determine the child's potential for growth.

What, exactly, does that mean? Well, the truth is, we don't really know. The Office of Special Education Programs released an FAQ on the *Endrew* ruling and that issue is not addressed. So, we'll take it at face value. First, it suggests a strengths-based approach in that it implies that every child has the potential for growth. That's a good thing. Second, in aligning this with the development of the IEP, one presumes that the PLAAFP needs to provide information about a child's potential for growth. So, what can we do to bring that to fruition?

One more comment on testing before we consider assessments that align with determining potential for growth and supporting personalizable education. I mentioned that I'm not going to talk about testing and assessment for diagnosis. I believe that a supports paradigm, where we consider the support needs of all children, can move us beyond having to diagnose and classify students and toward a system that provides needed instruction and supports to all students. That said, even within such a system, assessments that provide diagnostic information are helpful. While, in my opinion, IQ tests provide little or no helpful information pertaining to instruction, assessments that identify conditions like dyslexia or language/auditory processing difficulties have a role in planning and designing instruction and, if appropriate, therapy.

I have come to understand that even when the diagnostic information has limited helpful instructional implications, there are some benefits to diagnosis. A student I taught in the 1980s had, by her mother's report, developed pretty typically until between 1 and 2 years of age, when she began to lose motor functioning and language skills. She was an adolescent when I taught her, and she had quite extensive cognitive limitations, walked mainly on her toes, had no verbal communication skills, and constantly rubbed her hands together. Many of you will immediately recognize that this young woman had Rett syndrome, but in the early 1980s, the condition was not well known. (It first had been described by Andreas Rett in 1966, but described only in German publications, so until an English-language article was published in 1983, it was essentially unknown in the United States.)

Knowing when she was very young that this student had Rett syndrome might have had meaningful implications for early education and therapies, but it would not have changed the instruction I provided as her teacher. I had left my role as a teacher and was pursuing a master's degree at the University of Sussex in Brighton, England, when I received a letter and some pamphlets from this student's mother. In the letter, she described how her daughter had been diagnosed with Rett syndrome. It was a huge relief to her that the uncertainty surrounding the cause of her daughter's dramatic developmental change could be explained. Despite all logic, she had kept an underlying level of guilt that perhaps it was something she and her husband had done—a shot or vaccination was what she mentioned most—that had caused this outcome. The diagnosis was a relief to them, and it gave her a community of people who had shared life experiences. The diagnosis was a good thing for her.

MEASURING WHAT MATTERS, COUNTING WHAT COUNTS

So, what types of assessments will be important if we are to support personalizable learning and enable students with disabilities to navigate the 21st century. I've titled this section based on two documents in front of me at the moment: *Counting What Counts: Reframing Education Outcomes*, edited by my colleague Yong Zhao (2016), and the February 2018 issue of *Educational Leadership*, the theme in which was Measuring What Matters. In *Counting What Counts*, Yong Zhao and his co-authors argue that the "new paradigm of education should be about the individual," which is "a radical departure from the traditional paradigm that is about the group and the average" (p. 39). To make the shift, we must "reconsider the role and significance of talents and skills that have been traditionally undervalued" (p. 42).

Remember from Chapter 3 that in *Reach for Greatness: Personalizable Education for All Children*, Yong Zhao (2018) suggested that "the education system rarely cares about the children's individual passions or talents"(p. 17)? Zhao continued that thought by noting that "with very few exceptions, schools generally do not ask what students are good at, interested in, or passionate about" (p. 17). If we are to prepare young people for a future that is characterized by the importance of communication, creation, critical thinking, and collaboration, and are to embrace the idea that all children can be great in their own ways and that all talents are worth developing and passions worth pursuing, how does that change what we measure? How can we use assessment to measure what is needed in order to determine each child's potential for growth?

If we want to have student curiosity, passions, and strengths be the driving force for designing classrooms, schools, schedules, routines, curricula, and schools, then we have to find ways to measure student passions and strengths. If we want to promote agency, we have to find ways to measure student beliefs and self-determination. If the future requires students to be effective communicators, creators, critical thinkers, and collaborators, we need to find ways to measure those Four Cs.

In *Counting What Counts*, Yong Zhao contrasts new and traditional paradigms of assessment and educational outcomes. The first dichotomy, *homogenizing versus diversifying*, reflects the fact that the traditional paradigm assesses "the success of homogenization: how well all the students have mastered the set of skills, or content, or developed the desired qualities as prescribed in curriculum or standards" (p. 170). Assessment under a new paradigm, Zhao argues, must evaluate "how education contributes to enhancing individuals' talents" (p. 171), recognizing that every child is unique, that students' interests and abilities are diverse, and that what matters is assessing student growth, rather than comparing students with an average or with other students.

The second dichotomy is *short-term instruction versus long-term education*. Zhao (2016) suggests that "typically, students are assessed during or at the end of a course to appraise how many of the objectives of the course they have achieved," and that "the degree to which students master the predetermined content . . . is used as evidence of the students' learning outcomes and their abilities" (p. 171). Zhao reviews research, however, suggesting that this incremental "teach and test" method is detrimental to the development of children's creativity and curiosity, and that in emphasizing assessment of short-term gains, the traditional paradigm may sacrifice long-term educational outcomes critical for the 21st century.

Next, Zhao contrasts a traditional emphasis on cognitive skills with the need for a focus on noncognitive skills. This *cognitive versus noncognitive* skills dichotomy is emphasized frequently in discussions about education for the future. It is not that cognitive skills are not important. We've discussed the importance of critical thinking skills already. It is that most assessment and instruction is about the student's ability to memorize or follow directions, about a student's "ability to do certain things in a certain way" (2016, p. 173). Zhao notes that "very rarely are noncognitive domains such as motivation, persistence, confidence, and personality traits included in formal assessments" (p. 173). Finally, one of the reasons that we default to using measurements of short-term versus long-term outcomes and cognitive versus noncognitive skills is that what traditionally is measured are factors that are more easily quantified and counted. It is easier to measure a student's performance on a worksheet than to measure how that student's motivation might impact learning.

I've worked mostly in the realm of adolescent education and adolescent development, and when the high-stakes testing regime of No Child Left Behind came on to the national scene, one concern those of us in the field of transition services had was that important transition and school-to-work and life outcomes were going to be marginalized because these were not part of the "core content" being tested on statewide tests. Why were they not? I know there are many reasons, but would argue that most people believe these kinds of school-to-life skills are important, so that wasn't one of the reasons. At least one reason they're not assessed on annual high-stakes tests is that these skills are harder to measure. The *measurable versus unmeasurable* dichotomy reflects the reality that if what we measure matters more than what we don't measure, and if some outcomes are harder to measure than others, we may end up saying that what matters is what we are able to measure!

What, then, assessment practices might provide some direction for our work? Zhao (2016) identifies principles for a new paradigm, derived from these dichotomies, that include the importance of *personalization, long-term orientation, authenticity,* and *collaboration.* Personalization as a principle should not be a surprise. It is based upon what we've discussed with regard to going beyond individualization to promote agency and shared ownership of learning. As Yong Zhao (2016) notes:

> If we accept the premise that every individual is unique and all unique talents are worth developing and cultivating, enhancement of individual differences has to become a celebrated educational outcome, and such an education can only be realized first through personalization. (p. 176)

Keep in mind that what we're talking about here is personalization of the outcomes of education, not only the process. That is the gist of taking a long-term rather than a short-term orientation to assessment. Sure, we need data to drive instructional decisions on a day-to-day basis, and, as I'll discuss momentarily, I think we have a pretty good handle on what that might look like. But those data need to be in service of longer-term outcomes that are driven by student passions, interests, strengths, and abilities.

Further, assessment must inform and lead to value creation, which you'll recall from Chapter 3 refers to the active, engaged process of identifying learning needs that align with a student's curiosity and enabling students to turn their passions and strengths into something of value to them and others. And, of course, assessment in some way must inform efforts to support the development of collaboration skills in ways that individual measures of standardized performance simply do not.

What if we take as our marching orders, in responding to the Supreme Court's *Endrew* decision, to adopt this broader agenda to create an educational system that focuses on student potential for growth? What if we look not only at strengths, but assume that students are likely to grow in areas that they are interested in, have passion for, and feel they are capable in? What if we work as hard at measuring student strengths and interests as we do at measuring student deficits? Remember the quote from positive psychologist Chris Peterson I used in Chapter 1? He defined positive psychology as "the 'scientific' study of what makes life most worth living . . . a call for psychological science and practice to be as concerned with strength as with weakness: as interested in building the best things in life as in repairing the worst" (Peterson, 2009, p. xxiii).

Under even the kindest evaluation of how we use assessment with students with disabilities, it is difficult to see how we have been concerned as much about strengths as about weaknesses. Too often, we have been about repairing what is worst about students.

I'll talk more about the role of promoting self-determination in Chapter 8, but having developed several measures of self-determination for use with students with disabilities over the years, I am keenly aware of the relative lack of measures that focus on strengths or interests of students with disabilities. Almost every time I've wanted to measure something from the realm of positive psychology with students with disabilities—from measuring hope and optimism to student agency to perceptions of empowerment—I have had to first evaluate the psychometrics of those instruments with that population because that had not been done before.

In fact, there are assessments in positive psychology that measure hope, courage, positive emotions, positive human characteristics leading to positive work outcomes, positive coping, well-being, life satisfaction, optimism, problem solving, creativity, and on and on. And, these tools are being used increasingly in education. But, they are not developed with students with disabilities in mind and are not being used in special education.

My colleague at the University of Kansas, Karrie Shogren, and I have worked with the VIA Classification of Strengths as a means to focus on strengths for youth with disabilities. We've created a supplemental guide to the implementation of the VIA Inventory of Strengths for Youth that supports its use with adolescents with intellectual and developmental disabilities. The VIA measures character strengths in six domains: wisdom, courage, humanity, justice, temperance, and transcendence, within which are clustered 24 individual character strengths. So, I ask, how many students do you know who have a section of their PLAAFP that reports measures of kindness, optimism, fairness, forgiveness, creativity, or bravery? How many students have goals written based upon their appreciation of beauty and excellence, their social intelligence, or their curiosity? We have a cottage industry that assesses deficits and defects.

We have made some progress in recent years in the field with regard to measuring strengths. Our own work in promoting self-determination has resulted in several instruments that provide information on student self-determination and information for growth in that area (see www.self-determination.org for more information). At least in the area of intellectual and developmental disabilities, there has been a focus on the importance of quality of life. But, we have a long way to go in both validating and creating measures that inform practice around agency, creativity, collaboration, and strengths for students with disabilities.

ASSESSING POTENTIAL FOR GROWTH

In Chapter 2, I talked about our work on the Supports Intensity Scale measures as a way to replace measures of personal deficits (like intelligence tests) and provide information that might be useful for determining the need for specially designed instruction (the first purpose of the PLAAFP) as well as provide information that is useful in designing supports and providing instruction. The second function of the PLAAFP, as we've discussed, is to provide information for goals to be set in the IEP.

Let me choose as an area of consideration in how we use measures now, the use of achievement tests to provide information for the PLAAFP. I do acknowledge that achievement tests are one way to provide information about a student's present level of academic achievement in specific content areas. Achievement tests can be criterion-referenced in that they measure student performance compared with an existing or predetermined standard (e.g., grade, age, etc.) or norm-referenced, in that they provide information about a student's percent ranking compared with the population against whom the measure was normed.

Whatever their form, achievement tests tell us where students are in comparison with something or someone else. Are we going to get where we need to go in determining a student's potential for growth solely by comparing it with a standard or with the potential of others? A lot of the PLAAFP sections I have reviewed in my years read like a litany of information comparing a student's performance with grade- or age-level standards or with a normative sample, usually emphasizing the student's deficits.

Where does that leave us in determining a student's potential for growth? If we determine all of a student's goals on assessments based on homogenization, to use Yong Zhao's word, where do we find the information we need to create a personalizable education for every student? Personally, I think the Supreme Court's requirement that we build students' education around their potential for growth has to go well beyond simply determining how students are performing currently compared with standards or other students.

How do we do that? Well, we need to begin by rising to the challenge to create or validate measures focused on strengths, life satisfaction, creativity, collaboration, and so forth. They exist; we just don't use them much. And we need to use them in determining student educational goals.

As I mentioned before, I think we have strategies that get us information about potential for growth on a day-to-day basis. We've discussed the importance of schoolwide applications in 21st-century educational systems. One practice to emerge out of the Response to Intervention process has been progress monitoring, which involves frequent and repeated assessments of student learning and performance that, when charted or graphed, provide information about progress. The focus on change when students are not progressing adequately involves changes to the intensity or type of instruction.

But really, progress monitoring helps us track how students are doing on already determined tasks. We have to ask how we can we enable students to track their own progress to promote agency. Special education professors

Nancy Frey and Doug Fisher and researcher John Hattie (2018), whose efforts to synthesize the evidence for a variety of educational practices has had wide impact, talk about developing "assessment capable" learners (p. 47). I'm not real keen on that term, but I think they are on target with regard to their intent. They are asking how we move from assessment as something we do to students, to assessment as something that students have agency over. They identify an "assessment capable student" as a student who:

- Is aware of their current level of understanding in a learning area.
- Understands their learning paths and are confident enough to take on the challenge.
- Can select tools and resources to guide their learning.
- Seeks feedback and recognizes that errors are opportunities to learn.
- Monitors their own progress and adjusts course as needed.
- Recognizes what they are learning and can teach others. (Frey et al., 2018, p. 47)

Again, we'll talk more about how to move beyond teaching and dependency to promote student autonomy and self-determination in the next two chapters. Those provide some direction for achieving the goal of utilizing assessment that drives agency and shared ownership.

In addition to focusing on personalization and promoting agency, how do we take a long-term orientation to assessment? I think we broaden the focus of assessment from achievement and performance (remember that PLAAFP stands for "present level of academic achievement and functional performance") to embrace assessments of social–emotional learning and so-called noncognitive or soft skills, by measuring motivation and student interests and preferences, and using assessments that "help us learn about students—not to sort them" (Milner, 2018, p. 88).

In discussing the development of assessment for equity, Milner (2018) noted that

> We should be working toward assessments . . . that help us improve our practices to support student growth and diversity. These assessments may be written, oral, performative, arts-centered, or technologically enhanced. (pp. 88–89)

Milner suggests that such assessments should:

1. Be used to gauge student learning, development, and improvement over time.
2. Be used by teachers to adjust their practices.
3. Not intimidate students, but enable them to see assessment as opportunities to improve what they want and need to improve.
4. Be just as diverse as students themselves. (p. 89)

I think we actually know some of how to do this. What Milner is talking about involves elements of MTSS and progress monitoring, Universal Design for Learning, self-determination, and self-directed learning, and reflects the importance of equity that is valued by most special educators.

DYNAMIC LEARNING MAPS

I didn't want to leave the topic of going beyond testing without touching on the potential for technology to open up our capacity to assess in ways that promote growth and mastery instead of performance and achievement. In 2010, the U.S. Department of Special Education's Office of Special Education Programs funded two large projects to come up with better alternative assessments for students with the most significant cognitive disabilities. Colleagues in the Achievement and Assessment Institute (AAI) at the University of Kansas received one of these projects, and I had the opportunity to serve in an advisory capacity, an experience that broadened my understanding of the potential for technology to change how we do assessment. The researchers at AAI adopted a "learning maps" model for the development of assessment. You can learn more about this model at www.dynamiclearningmaps. org, but think of it this way: Our brain consists of a network of interconnected neurons. In many cases, when one part of the brain is injured, and a particular pathway of neurons disrupted, the neurons in our brain reconnect in other ways that enable the function supported in the injured part of the brain to continue. This is called parallel distributed processing.

The Dynamic Learning Maps (DLM) consortium, as the AAI work was called, recognized that learning can work the same way. We mostly think of learning as a linear process. We learn skill A, which leads to skill B, which leads to skill C, which leads to skill D, and so forth. If, for any reason, a student cannot acquire skill B, that student's journey to skill C or D stops. What the DLM model recognized was that, like the brain, there are multiple paths to learning, and that if a student cannot acquire skill B, there is probably a B1 or a B2 or a B3 skill that will keep that student moving forward and potentially lead to skill C (or C1 or C2 or C3) and ultimately to skill D.

The DLM folks talk about this in terms of a map. If one road on your journey to your destination is blocked, you find another route that can get you to the same destination. The DLM team members have identified thousands of "nodes," which are individual concepts and skills associated with learning to read, do math, or do science. Using Bayesian statistical models that predict relationships, they have developed a learning map that describes the routes (skill B, B1, B2, etc.) to the destination of successful learning.

The DLM assessment is online and allows teachers to assess student progress and to determine a roadmap, based upon student strengths and already-learned skills, leading to student progress. Keep in mind that this was developed for use with students with the most extensive support needs—students for whom reading, math, and science rarely have been considered viable outcomes. Further, the DLM team is working to extend its maps to be viable for all students and to go beyond achievement in only these domains.

DETERMINING WHAT MATTERS MOST

I began this chapter noting the link between assessment and instruction. I think it is true that we need to know what students know before we design instruction. But, Carol Ann Tomlinson, whose work established the importance of differentiated instruction, observes that before we decide how to measure, we need to decide what matters most. As did Yong Zhao, Tomlinson (2018) observes that right now we tend to measure students' "capacity to store, retrieve, and repeat bits of information and skills too often devoid of meaning" (p. 90). We need, Tomlinson suggests, to "think deeply about what it is that really does matter most in learning" (p. 90).

CHAPTER 7

Beyond Teaching

Autonomy-Supportive Classrooms and Motivating Students

Specially designed instruction is defined in IDEA as "adapting, as appropriate to the needs of an eligible child, the content, methodology, or delivery of instruction to address the unique needs of the child that result from the child's disability and to ensure access of the child to the general curriculum, so that the child can meet the educational standards within the jurisdiction of the public agency that apply to all children" [34 CFR §300.39(b)(3)].

Some people seem to focus on accommodations and modifications as the defining features of specially designed instruction, but I think (and I think the IDEA definition of specially designed instruction supports this) that it's really about personalizing instruction so learners can learn. It is, really, at the heart of what it means to be a special educator. It is about teaching.

So why in the world would we need to go "beyond teaching" if we are to provide high-quality educational experiences for students with disabilities? In Chapter 5, I mentioned that learning theory in distance education and online learning was moving us from pedagogy to heutagogy, and I want to revisit those ideas and then talk about how we provide education that motivates students and promotes agency and shared ownership in learning. Recall that I quoted from a researcher in the area of online and distance learning who said:

> Pedagogical, even andragogical, educational methods are no longer fully sufficient in preparing learners for thriving in the workplace, and a more self-directed and self-determined approach is needed, one in which the learner reflects upon what is learned and how it is learned and in which educators teach learners how to teach themselves. (Blaschke, 2012, p. 57)

Certainly, this is consistent with moving beyond individualization to personalizable education. I'm going to talk about self-determination and self-determined learning in the next chapter; strategies that, as Blaschke suggested, teach learners how to teach themselves. We begin, though, by thinking beyond just teaching, to how we structure environments and provide instruction in ways that promote autonomy and agency.

BEYOND LIFE JACKETS

There is compelling research suggesting that promoting student voice and choice can result in some surprising results. One of my favorite studies was one that focused on choice and eating vegetables. The researchers set up an experiment in the cafeteria of an elementary school. One third of the children were assigned to a group that had to eat whatever vegetable (zucchini or green beans) was given to them. The other two-thirds of children were divided into two groups that could choose which vegetable they wanted to eat. All children could eat all they wanted. The children in one choice group could have second helpings of only the vegetable they chose originally, while children in the other choice group could choose to eat whatever they wanted the second time around. It turns out that children in both of the choice groups ate twice the amount (in grams) of vegetables than the children in the no-choice group (Dominguez et al., 2013).

Choice is motivating to students. Students are more likely to work on goals that are set based upon their interests and preferences and that they have a voice in setting. Heck, another study showed that simply allowing students to choose which homework they completed improved motivation, homework completion, and scores on tests linked to the homework (Patall & Hooper, 2018).

But, it is more than just the act of choosing that is motivating to students; it is the perception that they have autonomy. Let me talk a minute about what is intended by the notion of autonomy and then talk about the types of ways in which teachers can interact with students that lead students to believe that they have greater autonomy.

We tend to think of autonomy as synonymous with independence. When thinking about promoting the autonomy of students, most educators consider how to increase the independent functioning and performance of students. There's nothing wrong with that, certainly, but the key to student agency is more than doing things independently. In addition to the sense of autonomy-as-independence, there is a meaning of the term that relates to acting based upon personal preferences, interests, and values. That is the idea of autonomy-as-volition. *Volition* is a word that refers to acting based upon conscious choice, which means acting intentionally to enable you to achieve goals related to your preferences and interests. In essence, acting volitionally does not mean just acting whichever way you want that feels good; it means acting intentionally driven by your preferences and interests.

This is important because there are lots of things in school that students cannot choose to do or not to do. Even when schools are structured based upon shared ownership, this likely will be true. Further, there are things that students need to learn that, in and of themselves, are not of particular interest or inspire passion, but that lead students to learning things that are driven by their passions and interests.

Sometimes, we can work in an actual choice that gives students more autonomy, such as selecting which version of homework a student does. But not always. So, the question becomes, how do we promote student autonomy-as-volition on a day-to-day basis when much of what happens in schools is prescribed?

Research in motivation using self-determination theory has shown that autonomy-supportive teaching promotes student perceptions of autonomy and enhances intrinsic motivation. Before I describe this, I think it is important that we recognize that much of what we do to students with disabilities in schools does not promote autonomy as either independence or volition, and instead results in dependency.

My colleague, Jim Martin, who is a pioneer in innovative practices to engage learners with disabilities in educational and transition planning, once asked the rhetorical question: If students floated in life jackets for 12 years, would they be expected to swim if the jackets were suddenly jerked away?" (Martin, Marshall, Maxson, & Jerman, 2016, p. 4). Well, of course not. But, Martin and colleagues argued, that is exactly what happens in far too many cases in the education of learners with disabilities. They are placed in "programs" that result in dependence rather than autonomy. And, simply the way that students are taught often limits autonomy.

I suspect this will not be a universally popular opinion, so let me lay this out piece by piece. First, let's go back to the discussion about programs and segregation. One of the justifications for segregated settings is that it allows resources (people, equipment, etc.) to be focused on the students who need them the most and thus is more economical and advantageous. But, having been a classroom teacher in self-contained classrooms for adolescents with extensive support needs through much of the 1980s, I can say from experience that when one has a dozen or so students who all need something done for them (coat put on, backpack readied, materials located, etc.), it becomes difficult to support students to do these things as independently as they can. You end up doing things for students, even if you know they'd be better off doing the bits they could do on their own.

One of the so-called "characteristics" of people with intellectual disability identified through research in the 1960s and 1970s was that they are "outer-directed." That was a way of describing the fact that often students with intellectual disability would wait on someone (usually a teacher) to provide a cue before they performed a task, even when they could perform the task independently. The deficits model of disability led to the attribution of this as a characteristic of the individual. But really, it is a characteristic of the instruction that was provided. Essentially, people with intellectual disability "learned" to be prompt-dependent.

Why? Well, it turns out that there are analyses of the conditions that lead to prompt-dependency in the literature and that it is—well, complicated. It has to do with, mainly, ineffectiveness in withdrawing (fading) prompts or using overly intrusive prompts, the inadvertent delivery of prompts, issues pertaining to reinforcement schedules and reinforcement of differential responses, and so forth.

Just to be clear, I do not intend to engage in a critique of behavioral techniques here. I'm not Noam Chomsky. The application of operant principles to instruction was among the earliest strategies that showed that students with intellectual disability could learn if provided systematic instruction. I think any behaviorists worth their salt have to acknowledge the potential of prompt-dependency when prompting and reinforcement strategies are not appropriately used. But, I worry that, for whatever reason, far too many students with disabilities receive instruction that results in prompt-dependency. Add in the issues discussed previously around dependency-creating elements of segregated environments, and it becomes a problem.

As I've worked to promote self-determination, the unintended consequences of dependency created by the special education system have become more evident to me. Prompt-dependent is pretty much the opposite of self-determined or agentic or volitional.

Is this an issue just for students with more extensive cognitive support needs? I don't really think so. Consider an analysis of direct instruction provided by a colleague, Dennis Mithaug. Dennis begins by recognizing that direct instruction has a solid evidence base for success in teaching students who have difficulty learning, particularly when used over time with students with learning disabilities. Direct instruction is successful for two reasons. First, responses are learned when they come under the control of an instructional cue. Second, this relationship is strengthened when a reinforcing consequence is contingent upon correct responses to that cue. Thus, as Mithaug noted, "the more often an instructional cue is followed by a response that in turn is reinforced, the more likely it is that learning will occur" (Mithaug, Mithaug, Agran, Martin, & Wehmeyer, 2003, p. 41).

Mithaug argued that this interplay between teacher cues and student responses during direct instruction explains why it is effective and why it is limiting:

> Direct instruction is effective because optimizing learning opportunities for students (e.g., teacher cues) eliminates the need for them to improve their adjustments in order to learn. However, it is limiting for that reason, too. Direct

instruction eliminates the need for them to improve their adjustment capabilities, which inadvertently encourages their dependence on teachers for the optimization of difficult challenges. (Mithaug et al., 2003, p. 206)

Here's what Mithaug is pointing out. Even if students are not becoming prompt-dependent, they are not learning how to respond to their environment and to adjust their responses in the absence of explicit teacher cues.

Again, I'm not intending to pick a fight with applied behavior analysis or direct instruction. In fact, some of the strategies I'll talk about in the next chapter to promote self-determination are based upon behavioral principles. I do think, however, that this is something that we need to be vigilant about in the education of learners with disabilities, and I don't think we are. If we want to increase agency, it behooves us to know what teaching practices might promote such agency and autonomy.

AUTONOMY-SUPPORTIVE TEACHING

As I mentioned, research in motivation has explored what is referred to as autonomy-supportive teaching. That's autonomy-as-volition. Let's focus on two elements of autonomy-supportive teaching: arranging the context to promote autonomy and interacting with students in ways that promote autonomy. And although I probably don't have to say it, I'm referring to contexts and interactions in typical classrooms, not in separate classrooms.

In a book that Yong Zhao and I have written examining the role of self-determined learning in personalizable education, we've identified a number of elements of the classroom environment or context that can promote greater autonomy and perceptions of autonomy. These include:

- Organize and design the classroom to maximize student active engagement and participation.
- Make needed materials or learning resources available for students to access easily.
- Create learning centers that emphasize various talents and preferences instead of just topics.
- Provide supports for all students to participate (e.g., digital books as well as print books, properly sized tables).
- Expressly provide spaces and structure where students can explore and pursue their passions.
- Ensure that students have meaningful roles in setting classroom rules and feel safe to explore and take risks. (Wehmeyer & Zhao, in press)

We've already discussed the importance of Universal Design for Learning. The curriculum, of course, is part of the educational context, and teacher use of universally designed curricular materials augments classroom contexts to promote autonomy.

Most of the work in autonomy-supportive classrooms has looked at teacher style or teacher interactions with students. Johnmarshall Reeve (2002) has studied teachers and their interactions with students and concluded:

> Autonomy-supportive teachers distinguished themselves by listening more, spending less time holding instructional materials such as notes or books, giving students time for independent work, and giving fewer answers to the problems students face. (p. 186)

Reeve (2002) has identified autonomy-supportive teachers as teachers who:

- get to know the cognitive, social, and affective needs of each of their students.
- create opportunities for students to get to know one another.
- develop, maintain, and use a consistent and sustainable system of collecting information about individual student and group performance that will help them make informed grouping decisions throughout the year.
- support students in working together for multiple outcomes.
- understand and perform their role with learning groups as a coach, understanding the abilities and areas of needed support for each student.
- ensure that every student, regardless of age or ability level, receives and talks about success and progress each day.

IT'S ABOUT RELATIONSHIPS

Self-determination theory is intended to address the question of why we act volitionally. What factors motivate us to act based upon our preferences, interests, and passions? The theory suggests that humans are motivated to fulfill basic psychological needs for autonomy, competency, and relatedness. Autonomy refers, as we've discussed, to people's need to engage in activities that are autonomously motivating. The need for competency refers to the need of all people to believe they are capable and competent. The need for relatedness refers to people's need to feel connected with others and to feel a sense of social belonging (Ryan & Deci, 2017).

We've already talked in previous chapters about a lot of the elements of promoting students' perceptions of competency: a focus on strengths, mastery goals over performance goals, growth over competition. And, we've talked some about the importance of relatedness, but maybe not enough. Niemiec and Ryan (2009) state that, in schools, "relatedness is deeply associated with a student feeling that the teacher genuinely likes, respects, and values him or her" (p. 139).

By creating autonomy-supportive classrooms and engaging in autonomy-supportive teaching, teachers establish a foundation upon which competency and relatedness supports can be built and can enhance student autonomous motivation and agency. The next step is to provide instruction to teach students skills that enable them to become self-determined learners, and that is the focus of the next chapter.

CHAPTER 8

Beyond Dependency

Self-Determination and Self-Determined Learning

I talked about dependency in the previous chapter and how we begin to build autonomy-supportive contexts, engage in autonomy-supportive teaching, and promote autonomous motivation of students with disabilities to counter the dependency-creating elements of special education. I want to continue that theme in this chapter. Those of you who know my research and intervention work over the years will not be surprised that two of the chapters in this book focus on self-determination.

In 1988, the U.S. Department of Education's Office of Special Education Programs sponsored a conference on the then-unlikely topic of self-determination. Why unlikely? At the time of the conference, there was exactly one article that referenced self-determination in a peer-reviewed journal in the field of special education. That article was "The Importance of Motivation for the Future of the LD Field," written by self-determination theory founder Edward Deci and a colleague (Deci & Chandler, 1986).

The OSEP conference consisted of about 100 people, half of whom were people with disabilities (mainly young people) and half were people who supported (mainly young) people with disabilities, including researchers, teachers, siblings, and policymakers. I can tell you why the conference was held, although I'm not real clear on why "self-determination," per se, was the focus. As to the former, the conference was in response to a series of follow-up/follow-along studies conducted in the 1980s that examined adult outcomes for youth with disabilities. They found that although P.L. 94-142 was more than a decade old, employment and independent living outcomes were still pretty dismal for youth with disabilities. We'll come back to that in a moment, but with regard to the latter (why have a conference on "self-determination"?), the idea was that one of the factors contributing to poor transition outcomes for youth with disabilities was that students were not an integral part of the process.

The OSEP director at that time was Patricia McGill Smith, who was the parent of a child with more extensive support needs. The director of the OSEP Secondary Education and Transition Services branch was Dr. Michael Ward, who, as a man with cerebral palsy, had personal experience with disability. Both have told me that they identified self-determination as a focus. I tend to think that it was probably more Michael's doing, as his doctorate was in psychology and he would have had more familiarity with the term.

The conference could have focused, instead, on student involvement or student self-direction or self-regulation. As it turns out, at least in my opinion, a focus on self-determination was exactly what was needed because of the breadth of that construct. I believe that has been borne out today as we consider the types of skills that will be important for all young people in 2020 and beyond.

If Michael Ward and Patty McGill Smith were prescient with their identification of self-determination as of critical importance for the transition process, a Swedish philosopher named Bengt Nirje was clairvoyant at the level of Nostradamus. In 1972, Nirje, who had worked with adults with intellectual disability in the late 1960s to find ways to enable them to move out of institutions and into communities, published a chapter titled "The Right to Self-Determination." I still quote Nirje quite a bit because he nailed the importance of self-determination for all people. The chapter opens with the following:

> The choices, wishes, desires, and aspirations of a [handicapped] person have to be taken into consideration as much as possible in actions affecting him. To assert oneself with one's family, friends, neighbors, co-workers, other people, or vis-à-vis an agency is difficult for many persons. It is especially difficult for someone who has a disability or is otherwise perceived as devalued. But in the end, even the impaired person has to manage as a distinct individual, and thus has his identity defined to himself and to others through the circumstances and conditions of his existence. Thus, the road to self-determination is both difficult and all important for a person who is impaired. (Nirje, 1972, p. 177)

Take out the dated disability language and the gendered references, and Nirje's observation is as timely today as it was when it was published 3 years before P.L. 94-142 was passed. At the OSEP National Conference on Self-Determination, Robert Williams, who has personal experience with cerebral palsy and has been a leader in the federal government pertaining to disability for more than 4 decades, said the same thing in a different way:

> But, without being afforded the right and opportunity to make choices in our lives, we will never obtain full, first class American citizenship. So we do not have to be told what self-determination means. We already know that it is just another word for freedom. We already know that self-determination is just another word for describing a life filled with rising expectations, dignity, responsibility, and opportunity. That it is just another word for having the chance to live the American Dream. (Williams, 1989, p. 16)

One outcome of the National Conference on Self-Determination was that Michael Ward's OSEP Secondary Education and Transition Services branch funded a series of model demonstration projects to promote the self-determination of youth with disabilities. I had the good fortune to be hired as a project director for one of the first six projects. It's taken longer than I thought it would, but due to the work conducted through many of those projects and other federally funded research and demonstration projects, and as a result of the efforts of the people who worked on these and other initiatives (Sharon Field, Dennis Mithaug, Jim Martin, Brian Abery, Roger Stancliffe, and Laurie Powers, to name a few), promoting self-determination is now a "best practice" in secondary education and transition for youth with disabilities. We need to push this further than we have, though, and in this chapter I'll talk a bit about how we do that.

First, let me summarize very quickly what I and my colleagues mean when we talk about self-determination. Being self-determined means that you act volitionally to make or cause things to happen in your life. Volitional action refers to acting based upon conscious choice, as we talked about in the previous chapter. People who are self-determined are causal agents in their lives; they act with intent to achieve goals to act on their passions. My colleague Karrie Shogren and I, and our collaborators Susan Palmer, Todd Little, Shane Lopez, Anjali Forber-Pratt, and others, have built on theoretical and research work that began with that initial OSEP model demonstration project to propose causal agency theory to describe the causal action series that enables young people to act to fulfill basic psychological needs for autonomy, competency, and relatedness (see previous chapter) and enables students to be causal agents in their lives and become more self-determined (Shogren et al., 2015; Wehmeyer, Shogren, Little, & Lopez, 2017).

THE CONSEQUENCES OF DEPENDENCY

Let's take a minute to think about what successes we have had with regard to youth transition to adulthood, and whether we should just stay the course or whether we need to try something different. I was at a conference recently in which a state director of developmental disabilities services was talking about an innovative statewide initiative that was intended to promote greater independence and inclusion. As proof of the success of this initiative, this director pointed out that the employment rate for people with developmental disabilities in his state was nine percentage points above the national rate. Impressive, right? What was the national rate? Twenty-one percent. So 30% is the high bar we're trying to clear? I was, I must say, mainly discouraged. I've already mentioned (in Chapter 3) the Harris poll from 2010 that found the 21% employment rate and that one third of people with disabilities have household incomes of $15,000 or below.

One other outcome of the follow-up/follow-along studies from the 1980s that I mentioned previously was that there were a series of federally funded national transition outcomes studies, referred to as the National Longitudinal Transition Studies (NLTS). In 2010, the NLTS research team published a comparison across time of outcomes for youth with disabilities (Newman, Wagner, Cameto, Knokey, & Shaver, 2010). The report compares data across a 15-year period, from 1990 to 2005. There was good news. Postsecondary enrollment for youth with disabilities climbed 20%, from 26% to 46%. Employed youth were much more likely to receive paid vacation and benefits. Voter registration was up and volunteerism was up. So, let's celebrate the accomplishments and progress.

But, there were areas of ongoing concern. Employment rates, job duration, hours worked, and hourly wages were basically stagnant across that time. Students were not more likely to have a driver's license. The 2005 report showed that youth with disabilities were 11% more likely to have been arrested, compared with the 1990 report. Despite growth in postsecondary education enrollment, the gap between such enrollment by students with and without disabilities widened. And, if you break the results down by disability category, some youth (those with autism, those with intellectual disability) had even poorer outcomes.

It feels like we need to shake things up and try something different. What progress we've made is often countered by stagnation and regression. Unemployment remains unacceptably high for adults with disabilities. Far too many people with disabilities live in poverty. Depressingly, "Disability and Poverty" has its own Wikipedia page.

I think the ideas I've talked about with regard to personalizable education begin to shake things up in ways that might matter. In the area of transition to adulthood, to which the principles of personalizable education can be applied, of course, a movement toward a life design process is taking what I think Fullan and Zhao intend by deep learning and personalizable education, respectively, and applying it to the realm of what we call transition services.

CAREER CONSTRUCTION AND LIFE DESIGN

The Partnership for 21st Century Learning consortium, which we talked about in Chapter 3, has a focus on life and career skills. What 21st-century learners (and workers) need are skills related to flexibility and adaptability, initiative and self-direction, social and cross-cultural relationships, and productivity and accountability (www.p21.org/about-us/p21-framework/266-life-and-career-skills). The latter is closely linked to Yong Zhao's focus on value creation, and the role of product-oriented learning emphasized by

Fullan and colleagues for deep learning, flexibility, adaptability, initiative, self-direction—all of which are about self-determined learning, as we'll discuss in a moment.

I have worked with colleagues (Laura Nota, Salvatore Soresi, Lea Ferrari, Teresa Sgaramella, and Ilaria DiMaggio) at the University of Padua (in Italy, not too far from Venice) on issues pertaining to self-determination and students with disabilities. These colleagues are not special educators, but are vocational psychologists and career and vocational counselors. They have been at the forefront of a movement in the field of vocational and career counseling that I think has great potential for changing how we support students with disabilities to transition to adulthood and work and life. It is called the life design movement.

Life design emerged out of observations by scholar Mark Savickas, whose work on career construction and life design I discussed briefly in Chapter 3, that the fields of career counseling and vocational psychology were facing a crisis. Here's how Savickas and colleagues (2009) framed this:

> The core concepts of 20th century career theories and vocational guidance techniques must be reformulated to fit the postmodern economy. Current approaches are insufficient. First, they are rooted in assumptions of stability of personal characteristics and secure jobs in bounded organizations. Second, they conceptualize careers as a fixed sequence of stages. (p. 240)

Savickas identified implications of this changing landscape. Young people entering the work world today will likely occupy at least 10 (and probably many more) jobs (as opposed to a few secure jobs) over their lifetime. Savickas (2012) argued that "the new job market in an unsettled economy calls for viewing career not as a lifetime commitment to one employer, but as a recurrent selling of services and skills to a series of employers who need projects completed" (p. 13).

Career construction (Savickas, 2005) is the idea that given the implications of the 21st-century world of work, young people will have to "construct" their own careers. As Savickas (2005) said, "Careers do not unfold; they are constructed as individuals make choices that express their self-concepts and substantiate their goals in the social reality of work role" (p. 43).

The life design approach applies these notions of career construction to life in general. The life design approach "is framed as a lifelong self-construction process that aims to promote skills and competences in overall life planning" (Wehmeyer et al., in press). It embodies all of the features of how to respond to the 21st-century work and learning demands discussed in previous chapters in relation to personalizable education, and in this chapter in terms of the P21 career and life skills taxonomy.

SELF-DETERMINED LEARNING

Research in self-determination clearly has established that young people with disabilities who are more self-determined achieve more positive school and adult outcomes, including more positive employment and community integration outcomes, than their peers who are not as self-determined. I'll talk in a moment about the Self-Determined Learning Model of Instruction. If you go to www.self-determination.org, you can find a Teacher's Guide to that instructional model that provides links to this research.

This is all good. But I have come to believe that if we are to genuinely support students to construct their careers and design their lives, we're going to have to take the work in self-determination one step forward. This is best illustrated, I think, by going back to the evolution of adult learning that I introduced in Chapter 5. You'll recall that even as far back as the 1970s, theorists in adult education distinguished it from the strategies and approaches used to teach children (pedagogy) by emphasizing andragogy, or self-directed learning. Malcolm Knowles (1975), who coined the term *andragogy*, argued that learners "who take the initiative in learning, learn more things, and learn better, than do people who sit at the feet of teachers possibly waiting to be taught" (p. 14).

Self-direction in learning presumes that (1) learners are driven by a sense of curiosity; (2) life experiences are resources to be exploited to maximize learning; and (3) learners who are motivated internally will learn more effectively. Another researcher in adult learning identified the objectives of andragogy as facilitating learning to ensure that learners can conceive of goals and plans, exercise freedom of choice, follow through on actions to achieve goals and plans, exercise self-governance and self-discipline, and view themselves as autonomous (Candy, 1991).

I think those objectives capture what we've been working toward in efforts to promote the self-determination of youth with disabilities. And, those are all important learning characteristics and traits for 21st-century learners.

But, just as changing learning contexts and technology have forced adult education to move beyond andragogy to heutagogy, I think personalized education and life design require that we move beyond self-directed learning to self-determined learning. Recall that heutagogy means *discovered learning* and is referred to in the adult distance and online learning literature as self-determined learning. I think that those of us in special education (and certainly I've been guilty of this over time) have used self-determined learning and self-directed learning synonymously. I've always sort of thought of self-directed learning as the nuts and bolts of how we promote self-determination.

But, how are they different? Lisa Marie Blaschke (2012) from the Center for Open Education Research at the University of Oldenburg in Germany observed that while self-determined learning incorporates practices in self-directed learning, in self-determined learning the instructor "fully relinquishes ownership of the learning path and process to the learner, who negotiates learning and determines what will be learned and how it will be learned" (p. 59).

Ah. Sounds like personalizable education, right? If, as I think is true, an unintended consequence of how we teach students with disabilities is that they do not learn how to respond to their environment and to adjust their responses in the absence of explicit teacher or adult cues, what can we do to change that?

Dennis Mithaug was the lead author of a book we published titled *Self-Determined Learning Theory: Construction, Verification, and Evaluation* (Mithaug et al., 2003). The ideas in that book were, as I look at it now, trying to achieve the same objectives as those forwarded by researchers in adult learning with ideas pertaining to heutagogy. The gist of the book was that "student learning is maximized when student engagement produces optimal experiences to new challenges" (p. 3). The basic propositions forwarded by "self-determined learning theory" are that:

1. When learners perceive that an opportunity for learning in a circumstance is valuable to them (e.g., self-endorsed and congruent with values, interests, and passions) and manageable;
2. and when students have knowledge, beliefs, and experiences about their ability to self-regulate their actions to produce results (e.g., how to act as the causal agent in their lives);
3. then, students engage in the learning situations to optimize their adjustments and maximize their learning. (Mithaug et al., 2003, p. 3)

Recall adult learning theorist Lisa Marie Blaschke's observation that heutagogy requires a "more self-directed and self-determined approach . . . one in which the learner reflects upon what is learned and how it is learned and in which educators teach learners how to teach themselves" (p. 57). I was faced with this same issue in the mid-1990s as the work we were doing to understand self-determination began to move us toward creating interventions to promote self-determination. I had taken a college course on models of teaching in the early 1990s, and as I examined all of the models of teaching in the textbook I had used, I noted that they all focused on teaching teachers to teach students. Fair enough, that is exactly what pedagogy involves—teaching students.

But although I didn't have the language of andragogy and heutagogy at the time, I had the good fortune of having worked and talked with Dennis Mithaug, and the ideas that became the 2003 book on self-determined learning theory were already percolating.

I wasn't looking for a model to teach teachers to teach students. I was looking for a model to teach teachers to teach students to teach themselves. The framework for that model had been proposed by Dennis Mithaug, Jim

Martin, and Martin Agran in an article published in 1987. They were looking for a way to address the unemployment problem of young people with
disabilities—the same problem that precipitated the OSEP self-determination conference in 1988. They recognized that teaching students adaptability skills was the one thing missing from instruction to promote employment
up to that point. They framed the problem they were addressing in much the
same way I did in Chapter 7:

> The instructional approach that currently dominates nearly all programs for
> students with special learning needs assumes a level of student dependency that
> reinforces behaviors incompatible with independence and student initiative.
> Usually, the teacher provides direct instruction to students by personally de-
> livering instructional cues and consequences necessary to elicit and maintain
> correct responding. The teacher determines the schedule of tasks, reinforces the
> student immediately and directly, determines when the student should finish the
> next task, and directs the student to the next learning experience. (Mithaug et
> al., 1987, p. 501)

Mithaug et al. were all trained as behaviorists. They understood the
benefits and unintended consequences of direct and systematic instruction.
Their critique was not so much of direct instruction, but of the lack of recognition that instruction also needed to address the dependency-creating
aspects of this instructional modality. Their argument was that we needed
to teach students adaptability skills. Their solution was the Adaptability
Instruction Model, which focused on four elements: (1) decisionmaking, (2)
independent performance, (3) self-evaluation, and (4) adjustment.

When, in the mid-1990s, I was searching for a teaching model to enable
teachers to teach students to teach themselves, it struck me that the Adaptability Instruction Model had many of the elements that were needed, and
that if it could be expanded some, it might provide a model we could evaluate. So, in 1998, the three authors of the Adaptability Instruction Model,
my colleague Susan Palmer, and I got together in a retreat center on Pikes
Peak (Jim Martin and Dennis Mithaug were at the University of Colorado in
Colorado Springs at the time) and in 2-1/2 days hashed out what we called
the Self-Determined Learning Model of Instruction (SDLMI).

The premise of the SDLMI is fairly simple. If we expect young people
to teach themselves, we need to teach them to self-regulate problem-solving
processes that enable them to set learning goals, create action plans, and
track their progress toward the goals, revising their action plans or goals as
needed based upon their progress.

As I mentioned before, you can find more information on the SDLMI at
www.self-determination.org. Briefly, the SDLMI is implemented across three
phases. Each phase poses a problem for the student to solve: What is my
goal? What is my plan? and What have I learned? Teachers teach students to

solve these problems by answering a series of questions. These student questions vary by phase, but each phase comprises a four-step, problem-solving sequence. Aligned with each student question are teacher objectives, which basically describe what the teacher is trying to support the student to say and do in answering each question. Also listed with each teacher objective are educational supports that teachers may need to use to enable students to learn what they need in order to answer the question.

Instruction during phase 1 teaches students to solve the problem, "What is my goal?" and to define the discrepancy between what they know and what they want to know. The questions posed in this phase assist students to set a goal that will lead them to what they want to know. The last question in that phase asks: "What can I do to make this happen?" and students are supported to set a goal. In phase 2 students solve the problem, "What is my goal?" The questions in this phase support students to define the discrepancy between the action that is necessary in order to learn what they want to know and the actions they are capable of taking, and to engage in pathways thinking to create a plan. This phase ends with students having developed a plan of action and designing a self-monitoring process. In the third and final phase of the model, students solve the problem, "What have I learned?" and, in so doing, examine the discrepancy between their planned actions and the actions they've implemented, and between what they expected to learn and what they learned. Students use information they've gathered through their self-monitoring to self-evaluate progress and, supported by the questions in the phase, go through a decisionmaking process to determine whether their progress is sufficient (and, if so, keep working on it as they have been) or whether they need to alter their plan or goal.

What separates the SDLMI from other instructional approaches to promoting self-determination, I believe, is that it genuinely gives students ownership of their learning process. Students set goals, create plans, and learn to adjust their goals and plans. Teachers simply provide the instructional supports students need in order to move through the process. Again, this has nothing to do with students doing this completely independently, and everything to do with providing the supports that maximize student self-regulation of learning.

And, this is a model that all teachers could use to teach all students to self-regulate problem solving, set and attain goals, and become more self-determined. Led by Karrie Shogren, we currently are involved in a project that implements the SDLMI as a Tier 1 intervention for all students in inclusive high schools in Maryland and Delaware. Combine the SDLMI with the power of technology and universal design; mix in a healthy dose of student preferences, interests, and curiosity; stir in meaningful, value-creating projects and activities—and what I think you have is personalizable education.

Before I leave these issues of self-determination, I want to just comment on the current state of what we have called "student involvement" practices.

The 1990 reauthorization of IDEA introduced transition mandates, requiring that transition services be based upon student interests and preferences, taking into account student needs. It also required that when transition services were to be discussed in an IEP meeting, the student must be invited.

There is good evidence that using a variety of instructional strategies and programs, students with disabilities can learn to play a more meaningful role in their IEP meetings and that in so doing they become more self-determined. Again, all good. But the caution I have for this (which Jim Martin, whom I would credit as having come up with the idea of student-led IEPs, also has articulated) is that these activities are tied to an IEP meeting. That is a problem for two reasons. First, only students receiving special education services have IEPs, so that experience is not shared by students without disabilities. Second, the IEP meeting can be a source of tension and acrimony. Having students involved in such meetings in a meaningful way can defuse some of that, but there is still the possibility that the IEP meeting will be a disempowering process for the student.

Again, I'm not bashing the efforts to promote student involvement in IEPs. As long as we have IEPs, I think we need to work to put students at the center. But, we need to find a way to move beyond these disability-only experiences. Work by Scott Solberg and his colleagues, through the National Collaborative on Workforce and Disability for Youth, created a process called individualized learning plans (ILPs). Originally trying to improve upon the IEP process, Solberg and his colleagues have begun implementing the ILP process in a schoolwide manner, enabling all students to engage in the self-exploration, career exploration, and career-planning and management activities inherent in the ILP process (Solberg, Wills, Redmond, & Skaff, 2014). Importantly, Solberg also has worked with researchers in the life design movement, and the ILP process has promise to provide a means to enable students with and without disabilities to begin to learn how to design their own life and move beyond dependency.

Beyond Special Education

Educating All Learners in the 21st Century

I have reached this point in the book without saying something snarky about the word *special*, but maybe now is the time. A few years ago, John Lloyd from the University of Virginia asked me to write a chapter for a text he was editing with Barbara Bateman and Melody Tankersley titled *Enduring Issues in Special Education* (2015). Bateman, Lloyd, and Tankersley had structured the book's table of contents to address these "enduring issues" around topics pertaining to the who, what, where, when, why, and how of special education. I was asked to write a chapter for the "when" section, with the specific charge to talk about "when does special education end?"

The editors of this book provided me with quite a bit of latitude—they wanted me to end up talking about issues of self-determination, adult outcomes, living and working environments, and so forth. In my chapter, I noted that I could write about when eligibility for special education or specially designed instruction ends (age 22 in most states for some students), but that would miss the point. That point was:

> I want to take a step beyond special education eligibility or specially designed instruction and answer the question "When does special education end?" by discussing when the stigma and stereotypes that the term "special education" brings to the minds of most people, particularly the public, ends. (Wehmeyer, 2015, p. 369)

I made many of the same points I have made in this book—too many people think special education is a place to go or an adjective describing a student who has difficulty learning. What I believe to be the case is that the stigma associated with "special education" does not, in fact, ever end. It's why so many students with learning disabilities run as far away from being labeled (i.e., they don't disclose their disability) as they can when they get to college, even if it means they don't get some supports they need in order to succeed.

So, let's begin this final chapter, the Epilogue, by saying that we need to go beyond special education by dumping the term *special*. It is too laden with negative connotations to be salvaged. Let's just talk about how we educate learners with and without disabilities, that is, all learners, in the 21st century, shall we?

I began this book stating that it was written not as a critique of special education as it exists today, but with the intent to put forward some big ideas about how the education of learners with disabilities could be structured to meet 21st-century learning demands. So, what are those big ideas? How do we go beyond special education to educate all learners in the 21st century?

First, it is time to move *beyond disability*. We have better ways of thinking about how we educate all learners that take into account unique learning needs, whether or not students have a diagnosis or a disability. The person–environment fit model of disability places the experience of disability as a part of, and not apart from, typical human functioning, and the supports paradigm associated with that model provides us with a means to think about bridging the gap between a person's strengths and capacities and the demands of the environment. A disability/diagnosis focus leads to the creation of programs and services that tend toward homogeneous grouping and interventions predicated on deficits.

We need to go *beyond programs* and services to create a world-class education for all learners. I am captivated by Yong Zhao's ideas about reaching for greatness for all students: providing an education that addresses 21st-century needs for collaboration, communication, critical thinking, and creativity; that focuses on student agency, shared ownership, flexibility, and value creation; and that goes beyond individualization to create a personalizable education. We need to discard the idea of average as unhelpful to our efforts to educate all learners.

We need to go *beyond the continuum* to create whole-school systems that make the kinds of instructional expertise held by special educators available to support all students and, conversely, ensures that all students receive high-quality instruction in typical settings. We need to build schoolwide systems that focus on strengths, are driven by students' curiosity and passions, emphasize agency and shared ownership, create value, and encourage flexible mindsets. These are, fundamentally, inclusive communities. And, we need to do this in concert with general educators, not on our own.

Within these schoolwide systems, we need to go *beyond textbooks* and harness the power of technology and Universal Design for Learning to bolster the capacity of all students to act as agents in their own lives and to direct their own learning. We need to move from just teaching students to enabling students to self-direct learning using technology. Technology will allow us to promote student autonomy and agency, peer-to-peer learning, collaboration, and self-direction.

We need to go *beyond testing* to begin to measure what matters for the 21st century. We need to build the models and measures that allow us to identify how all children can be great, enable us to assess each student's potential for growth, identify each student's strengths, and move beyond homogenization to using assessment to inform and lead value creation and student agency.

We need to go *beyond teaching* to create autonomy-supportive classrooms that maximize student opportunities for choice and volitional action, and engage in autonomy-supportive teaching that promotes agency and supports student motivation by emphasizing students' curiosity and passions. We need to recognize that too much of what we do to students ends up minimizing student opportunities to learn how to respond in their environment and to adjust their responses in the absence of teacher or adult cues. When we focus on student strengths, student agency, mastery learning, and growth rather than competition, it allows us not only to create autonomy-supportive classrooms, but also to build relationships with students that show students we like, respect, and value them.

And, we need to go *beyond dependency* by promoting self-determination and teaching students to teach themselves; to become self-determined learners. We need to equip students with 21st-century skills to design careers and lives that enable them to live full, rich lives. We need to go beyond self-directed learning to enable students to engage in self-determined learning: to determine what to learn and how to learn it.

THIS BOOK had its genesis in my remarks at the OSEP celebration of the 40th anniversary of IDEA, as I mentioned in the Introduction. I was asked to look back at where we'd been, to examine where we were, and to explore where we needed to go next. Most of the big ideas I talked about at the OSEP celebration made it into this book, plus a few more.

I believe, personally, that the message and ideas in this book are achievable. Multi-tiered systems of supports are becoming commonplace, Universal Design for Learning is a well-known idea, positive behavior interventions and supports have been scaled up in many states and districts, and promoting self-determination is best practice in much of transition education. Much of what needs to change is attitudinal in nature. We need to change the lens through which we see the education of learners with disabilities.

For years I taught an introductory methods class in educating learners with more extensive support needs. The reality where I've lived and worked has been that these students have been educated mainly in segregated classrooms. The first thing I told the graduate students in that class, most of whom were already teaching or were para-educators, was that they were not responsible for what the education of their students looked like when they were hired, but they were responsible for what changed. I've always believed that change in schools happens from the teacher up. There will be barriers to achieving some of the practices in this book. But, if what we are doing isn't working, we have no other option than to try something else until we find what does work.

Each and every teacher can change how they interact with students with disabilities. We can discard the idea that some children will be below average, and begin to focus on each student's strengths. We can incorporate student voice and choice, structure our classrooms and our teaching to promote student agency and ownership of learning, and explore the use of technology to promote autonomy and self-determined learning. We can form alliances with other educators to create value in project-based learning and to implement whole-school innovations. None of these steps require major systems change. Often, they just require someone who is willing to think differently and look beyond disability: to go *beyond special education* to figure out how to educate all learners in the 21st century.

References

Abeson, A., & Zettel, J. (1977). The end of the quiet revolution: The Education for All Handicapped Children Act of 1975. *Exceptional Children, 44*, 115–128.

American Speech and Hearing Association. (2016). *2016 schools survey: SLP caseload characteristics report*. Rockville, MD: Author. Retrieved from www.asha.org/uploadedFiles/2016-Schools-Survey-SLP-Caseload-Characteristics.pdf

Baroff, G. S. (1974). *Mental retardation: Nature, cause, and management*. Washington, DC: Hemisphere.

Barry, D. (2016). *The boys in the bunkhouse: Servitude and salvation in the heartland*. New York, NY: Harper.

Bateman, B., Lloyd, J. W., & Tankersley, M. (Eds.). (2015). *Enduring issues in special education*. New York, NY: Routledge.

Batshaw, M.L. (1989). *Children with disabilities*. Baltimore, MD: Paul H. Brookes.

Benn, G. A. (2018). You don't know me like that! *Educational Leadership, 76*(1), 20–25.

Blaschke, L. M. (2012). Heutagogy and lifelong learning: A review of heutagogical practice and self-determined learning. *The International Review of Research in Open and Distance Learning, 13*, 56–71.

Candy, P. C. (1991). *Self-direction for lifelong learning*. San Francisco, CA: Jossey-Bass.

Carr, E. G., Horner, R. H., Turnbull, A. P., Marquis, J. G., McLaughlin, D. M., McAtee, M. L., . . . Doolabh, A. (1999). *Positive behavior support for people with developmental disabilities: A research synthesis*. Washington, DC: American Association on Mental Retardation.

Deci, E. L., & Chandler, C. L. (1986). The importance of motivation for the future of the LD field. *Journal of Learning Disabilities, 19*(10), 587–594.

Dilley, A., Fishlock, J., & Plucker, J. A. (2017). *What we know about communication*. Washington, DC: Partnership for 21st Century Learning.

Dilley, A., Kaufman, J. C., Kennedy, C., & Plucker, J. A. (2017). *What we know about critical thinking*. Washington, DC: Partnership for 21st Century Learning.

Dillon, R. (2018). Room for improvement. *Educational Leadership, 76*(1), 40–45.

Dominguez, P. R., Gamiz, F., Gil, M., Moreno, H., Zamora, R. M., Gallo, M., . . . de Brugada, I. (2013). Providing choice increases children's vegetable intake. *Food Quality and Preference, 30*, 109–113.

Erickson, A. S., Noonan, P. M., Brussow, J. A., & Gilpin, B. J. (2014). The impact of IDEA indicator 13 compliance on postsecondary outcomes. *Career Development and Transition for Exceptional Individuals, 37*(3), 161–167. doi: 10.1177/2165143413481497

Frey, N., Fisher, D., & Hattie, J. (2018). Developing "assessment capable" learners. *Educational Leadership, 75*(5), 47–51.

Fullan, M., Quinn, J., & McEachen, J. (2018). *Deep learning: Engage the world change the world.* Thousand Oaks, CA: Corwin.

Gartner, A., & Lipsky, D. K. (1987). Beyond special education: Toward a quality system for all students. *Harvard Educational Review, 57,* 367–395.

Jung, L. A., & Smith, D. (2018). Tear down your behavior chart! *Educational Leadership, 76*(1), 12–18.

Knowles, M. S. (1975). *Self-directed learning: A guide for learners and teachers.* Chicago, IL: Follett.

Lance, W. (1976). Who are *all* the children? *Exceptional Children, 43,* 66–76.

Luckasson, R., Borthwick-Duffy, S., Buntix, W.H.E., Coulter, D. L., Craig, E. M., Reeve, A., et al. (2002). *Mental retardation: Definition, classification, and systems of supports* (10th ed.). Washington, DC: American Association on Mental Retardation.

Luckasson, R., Coulter, D. L., Polloway, E. A., Reiss, S., Schalock, R. L., Snell, M. E., . . . Stark, J. A. (1992). *Mental retardation: Definition, classification, and systems of supports* (9th ed.). Washington, DC: American Association on Mental Retardation.

Martin, J., Marshall, L., Maxson, L., & Jerman, M. (2016). *Self-directed IEP: Teacher's manual* (3rd ed.). Norman, OK: Zarrow Center for Learning Enrichment.

Milner, H. R. (2018). Assessment for equity. *Educational Leadership, 75*(5), 88–89.

Mithaug, D. E., Martin, J. E., & Agran, M. (1987). Adaptability instruction: The goal of transitional programming. *Exceptional Children, 53*(6), 500–505.

Mithaug, D. E., Mithaug, D. K., Agran, M., Martin, J. E., & Wehmeyer, M. L. (2003). *Self-determined learning theory: Construction, verification, and evaluation.* Mahwah, NJ: Erlbaum.

National Association of State Directors of Special Education. (2005). *Response to intervention: Policy considerations and implementation.* Alexandria, VA: Author.

National Center for Learning Disabilities. (2018). *Agents of their own success: Self-advocacy skills and self-determination for students with disabilities in the era of personalized learning.* Washington, DC: Author. Retrieved from www.ncld.org/wp-content/uploads/2018/03/Agents-of-Their-Own-Success_Final.pdf

National Education Association. (2016). *Preparing 21st century students for a global society: An educator's guide to the "four Cs."* Washington, DC. Author.

National Research Council. (1999). *High stakes: Testing for tracking, promotion, and graduation.* Washington, DC: Author.

Newman, L., Wagner, M., Cameto, R., Knokey, A-M., & Shaver, D. (2010). *Comparisons across time of the outcomes of youth with disabilities up to 4 years after high school.* Washington, DC: Institute of Education Sciences, National Center for Special Education Research. Retrieved from nlts2.sri.com/reports/2010_09/nlts2_report_2010_09_execsum.pdf

Niemiec, C. P., & Ryan, R. M. (2009). Autonomy, competence, and relatedness in the classroom: Applying self-determination theory to educational practice. *Theory and Research in Education, 7,* 133–144.

Nirje, B. (1972). The right to self-determination. In W. Wolfensberger (Ed.), *Normalization: The principle of normalization* (pp. 176–200). Toronto, ON: National Institute on Mental Retardation.

Orkwis, R., & McLane, K. (1998). *A curriculum every student can use: Design principles for student access* (ERIC/OSEP Topical Brief). Reston, VA: Council for Exceptional Children.

Patall, E. A., & Hooper, S. Y. (2018). The role of choice in understanding adolescent autonomy and academic functioning. In B. Soenens, M. Vansteenkiste, & S. Van Petegem (Eds.), *Autonomy in adolescent development: Toward conceptual clarity* (pp. 145–167). London, UK: Routledge.

Peterson, C. (2009). Foreword. In C. R. Snyder & S. J. Lopez (Eds.), *Oxford handbook of positive psychology* (2nd ed., pp. xxiii–xxiv). Oxford, UK: Oxford University Press.

Plucker, J. A., Kennedy, C., & Dilley, A. (2017). *What we know about collaboration.* Washington, DC: Partnership for 21st Century Learning.

Reeve, J. (2002). Self-determination theory applied to educational settings. In E. L. Deci & R. M. Ryan (Eds.), *Handbook of self-determination research* (pp. 183–203). Rochester, NY: Rochester University Press.

Reinke, W. M., Herman, K. C., & Stormont, M. (2013). Classroom-level positive behavior supports in schools implementing SW-PBIS: Identifying areas for enhancement. *Journal of Positive Behavior Interventions, 15*(1), 39–50. doi: 10.1177/1098300712459079

Rose, D. H., & Meyer, A. (2002). *Teaching every student in the digital age: Universal design for learning.* Alexandria, VA: ASCD.

Ryan, R., & Deci, E. (2017). *Self-determination theory: Basic psychological needs in motivation, development, and wellness.* New York, NY: Guilford.

Sailor, W. (2002). *Whole school success and inclusive education: Building partnerships for learning, achievement, and accountability.* New York, NY: Teachers College Press.

Sailor, W., & Roger, B. (2005). Rethinking inclusion: Schoolwide applications. *Phi Delta Kappan, 86*(7), 503–509.

Sarason, S. B. (1985). *Psychology and mental retardation: Perspectives in change.* Austin, TX: PRO-ED.

Sarason, S. B. (1990). *The predictable failure of educational reform: Can we change course before it's too late?* San Francisco, CA: Jossey-Bass.

Sarason, S. B. (1996). *Revisiting "The culture of the school and the problem of change."* New York, NY: Teachers College Press.

Sarason, S. B. (1998a). *Charter schools: Another flawed educational reform.* New York, NY: Teachers College Press.

Sarason, S. B. (1998b). *Political leadership and educational failure.* San Francisco, CA: Jossey-Bass.

Savickas, M. L. (2005). The theory and practice of career construction. In S. D. Brown & R. W. Lent (Eds.), *Career development and counseling: Putting theory and research to work* (pp. 42–60). Hoboken, NJ: Wiley.

Savickas, M. L. (2012). Life design: A paradigm for career intervention in the 21st century. *Journal of Counseling & Development, 90,* 13–19.

Savickas, M. L., Nota, L., Rossier, J., Bauwalder, J-P., Duarte, M. E., Guichard, J., . . . van Vianen, A.E.M. (2009). Life designing: A paradigm for career construction in the 21st century. *Journal of Vocational Behavior, 75,* 239–250.

Schwab, K. (2017). *The fourth industrial revolution.* New York, NY: Crown Business.

Seligman, M.E.P., & Csikszentmihalyi, M. (2000). Positive psychology: An introduction. *American Psychologist, 55,* 5–14.

Shogren, K. A., Wehmeyer, M. L., Martinis, J., & Blanck, P. (2019). *Supported decision-making: Theory, research, and practice to enhance self-determination and quality of life.* Cambridge, UK: Cambridge University Press

Shogren, K. A., Wehmeyer, M. L., Palmer, S. B., Forber-Pratt, A., Little, T., & Lopez, S. (2015). Causal agency theory: Reconceptualizing a functional model of self-determination. *Education and Training in Autism and Developmental Disabilities, 50*(3), 251–263.

Snyder, C. R., & Lopez, S. J. (Eds.). (2009). *The Oxford handbook of positive psychology* (2nd ed.). Oxford, UK: Oxford University Press.

Solberg, V. S., Wills, J., Redmond, K., & Skaff, L. (2014). *Use of individualized learning plans as a promising practice for driving college and career readiness efforts: Findings and recommendations from a multi-method, multi-study effort.* Washington, DC: National Collaborative on Workforce and Disability for Youth, Institute for Educational Leadership. Retrieved from www.ncwd-youth. info/wp-content/uploads/2018/03/ILPs-A-Promising-Practice-for-Driving-College-and-Career-Efforts.pdf

Sugai, G., & Simonsen, B. (2012). *Positive behavioral interventions and supports: History, defining features, and misconceptions.* Storrs: University of Connecticut: Center for Positive Behavioral Interventions and Supports. Retrieved from www.pbis.org/common/pbisresources/publications/PBIS_revisited_June19r_2012.pdf

Thompson, J. R., Bradley, V. J., Buntinx, W.H.E., Schalock, R. L., Shogren, K. A., Wehmeyer, M. L., . . . Yeager, M. H. (2009). Conceptualizing supports and the support needs of people with intellectual disability. *Intellectual and Developmental Disabilities, 47,* 135–146.

Thompson, J. R., Bryant, B., Campbell, E. M., Craig, E. M., Hughes, C., Rotholz, D. A., . . . Wehmeyer, M. L. (2004). *The supports intensity scale.* Washington, DC: American Association on Intellectual and Developmental Disabilities.

Thompson, J. R., Wehmeyer, M. L., Hughes, C., Shogren, K. A., Seo, H., Little, T.D., . . . Tasse, M. J. (2016). *The supports intensity scale—Children's version.* Washington, DC: American Association on Intellectual and Developmental Disabilities.

Tinley, T. (2018). Finding your classroom's greatness. *Educational Leadership, 76*(1), 76–81.

Tomlinson, C. A. (2018). Measuring doesn't come first. *Educational Leadership, 75*(5), 90–91.

Truebridge, S. (2014). *Resilience begins with beliefs: Building on student strengths for success in school.* New York, NY: Teachers College Press.

Turnbull, R. (2019). Foreword: Emancipation from the dead hand of paternalism (pp. xxi–xxviii). In K. A. Shogren, M. L. Wehmeyer, J. Martinis, & P. Blanck, *Supported decision-making: Theory, research, and practice to enhance self-determination and quality of life.* Cambridge, UK: Cambridge University Press.

U.S. Department of Education. (2018). *39th annual report to Congress on the implementation of the Individuals with Disabilities Education Act.* Washington, DC: Office of Special Education Programs.

Vaughn, S., & Fuchs, L. S. (2003). Redefining learning disabilities as inadequate response to instruction: The promise and potential problems. *Learning Disabilities: Research & Practice, 18*(3), 137–146.

Voulgarides, C. K. (2018). *Does compliance matter in special education? IDEA and the hidden inequities of practice.* New York, NY: Teachers College Press.

Wehmeyer, M. L. (2013). *The Oxford handbook of positive psychology and disability.* Oxford, UK: Oxford University Press.

Wehmeyer, M. L. (2015). When does special education end? In B. Bateman, J. W. Lloyd, & M. Tankersley (Eds.), *Enduring issues in special education* (pp. 366–381). New York, NY: Routledge.

Wehmeyer, M. L., Nota, L., Soresi, S., Shogren, K. A., Morningstar, M., Ferrari, L., . . . Di Maggio, I. (in press). A crisis in career development: Life designing and implications for transition. *Career Development and Transition for Exceptional Individuals.*

Wehmeyer, M. L., Shogren, K. A. Little, T. D., & Lopez, S. J. (Eds.). (2017). *Development of self-determination through the life-course.* New York, NY: Springer.

Wehmeyer, M. L., & Zhao, Y. (in press). *Educating students to become self-determined learners: Why and how.* Alexandria, VA: ASCD.

Weintraub, F. J. (1977). Editorial comment. *Exceptional Children, 44,* 114.

Williams, R. R. (1989). Creating a new world of opportunity: Expanding choice and self-determination in lives of Americans with severe disability by 1992 and beyond. In R. Perske (Ed.), *Proceedings from the National Conference on Self-Determination* (pp. 16–17). Minneapolis, MN: Institute on Community Integration.

World Health Organization. (1980). *International classification of impairments, disabilities, and handicaps.* Geneva, Switzerland: Author.

World Health Organization. (2001). *International classification of functioning, disability, and health*. Geneva, Switzerland: Author.

World Health Organization. (2002). *Towards a common language for functioning, disability, and health (ICF)*. Geneva, Switzerland: Author.

Zhao, Y. (2012). *World class learners: Educating creative and entrepreneurial students*. Thousand Oaks, CA: Corwin.

Zhao, Y. (2016)(Ed.). *Counting what counts: Reframing education outcomes*. Bloomington, IN: Solution Tree Press.

Zhao, Y. (2018). *Reach for greatness: Personalizable education for all children*. Thousand Oaks, CA: Corwin.

Index

About the Author

Michael L. Wehmeyer is the Ross and Marianna Beach Distinguished Professor in Special Education, chair of the department of special education, and senior scientist and director of the Beach Center on Disability, University of Kansas.